Outsourcing

Other Books of Related Interest

Opposing Viewpoints Series
America's Global Influence
The Minimum Wage
Work and Family

At Issue Series
Are Executives Paid Too Much?
Corporate Corruption
Should the Federal Government Bail Out Private Industry?

Current Controversies Series
Consumer Debt
Fair Trade
Jobs in America

"Congress shall make
no law ... abridging
the freedom of speech,
or of the press."

First Amendment to the US Constitution

The basic foundation of our democracy is the First Amendment guarantee of freedom of expression. The Opposing Viewpoints Series is dedicated to the concept of this basic freedom and the idea that it is more important to practice it than to enshrine it.

Outsourcing

Jenny Cromie and Lynn M. Zott, Book Editors

GREENHAVEN PRESS
A part of Gale, Cengage Learning

Detroit • New York • San Francisco • New Haven, Conn • Waterville, Maine • London

Elizabeth Des Chenes, *Director, Publishing Solutions*

© 2013 Greenhaven Press, a part of Gale, Cengage Learning

Gale and Greenhaven Press are registered trademarks used herein under license.

For more information, contact:
Greenhaven Press
27500 Drake Rd.
Farmington Hills, MI 48331-3535
Or you can visit our Internet site at gale.cengage.com.

For product information and technology assistance, contact us at:

Gale Customer Support, 1-800-877-4253.
For permission to use material from this text or product, submit all requests online at www.cengage.com/permissions.

Further permissions questions can be emailed to permissionrequest@cengage.com.

Articles in Greenhaven Press anthologies are often edited for length to meet page requirements. In addition, original titles of these works are changed to clearly present the main thesis and to explicitly indicate the author's opinion. Every effort is made to ensure that Greenhaven Press accurately reflects the original intent of the authors. Every effort has been made to trace the owners of copyrighted material.

Cover image © Jose Luis Pelaez, Inc./Blend Images/Alamy.

LIBRARY OF CONGRESS CATALOGING-IN-PUBLICATION DATA

Outsourcing / Jenny Cromie and Lynn M. Zott, book editors.
    p. cm. -- (Opposing viewpoints)
    Includes bibliographical references and index.
    ISBN 978-0-7377-6064-4 (hbk.) -- ISBN 978-0-7377-6065-1 (pbk.)
    1. Contracting out. 2. Contracting out--Government policy--United States. I. Cromie, Jenny. II. Zott, Lynn M. (Lynn Marie), 1969-
    HD3860.O98 2013
    658.4'058--dc23

                                                                        2012036368

Printed in the United States of America
1 2 3 4 5 6 7 17 16 15 14 13

Contents

Why Consider Opposing Viewpoints?

> "The only way in which a human being
> can make some approach to knowing
> the whole of a subject is by hearing
> what can be said about it by persons of
> every variety of opinion and studying
> all modes in which it can be looked at
> by every character of mind. No wise
> man ever acquired his wisdom in any
> mode but this."
>
> *John Stuart Mill*

In our media-intensive culture it is not difficult to find differing opinions. Thousands of newspapers and magazines and dozens of radio and television talk shows resound with differing points of view. The difficulty lies in deciding which opinion to agree with and which "experts" seem the most credible. The more inundated we become with differing opinions and claims, the more essential it is to hone critical reading and thinking skills to evaluate these ideas. Opposing Viewpoints books address this problem directly by presenting stimulating debates that can be used to enhance and teach these skills. The varied opinions contained in each book examine many different aspects of a single issue. While examining these conveniently edited opposing views, readers can develop critical thinking skills such as the ability to compare and contrast authors' credibility, facts, argumentation styles, use of persuasive techniques, and other stylistic tools. In short, the Opposing Viewpoints Series is an ideal way to attain the higher-level thinking and reading skills so essential in a culture of diverse and contradictory opinions.

In addition to providing a tool for critical thinking, Opposing Viewpoints books challenge readers to question their own strongly held opinions and assumptions. Most people form their opinions on the basis of upbringing, peer pressure, and personal, cultural, or professional bias. By reading carefully balanced opposing views, readers must directly confront new ideas as well as the opinions of those with whom they disagree. This is not to argue simplistically that everyone who reads opposing views will—or should—change his or her opinion. Instead, the series enhances readers' understanding of their own views by encouraging confrontation with opposing ideas. Careful examination of others' views can lead to the readers' understanding of the logical inconsistencies in their own opinions, perspective on why they hold an opinion, and the consideration of the possibility that their opinion requires further evaluation.

Evaluating Other Opinions

To ensure that this type of examination occurs, Opposing Viewpoints books present all types of opinions. Prominent spokespeople on different sides of each issue as well as well-known professionals from many disciplines challenge the reader. An additional goal of the series is to provide a forum for other, less known, or even unpopular viewpoints. The opinion of an ordinary person who has had to make the decision to cut off life support from a terminally ill relative, for example, may be just as valuable and provide just as much insight as a medical ethicist's professional opinion. The editors have two additional purposes in including these less known views. One, the editors encourage readers to respect others' opinions—even when not enhanced by professional credibility. It is only by reading or listening to and objectively evaluating others' ideas that one can determine whether they are worthy of consideration. Two, the inclusion of such viewpoints encourages the important critical thinking skill of objectively evaluating an author's credentials and bias. This evaluation will illuminate an author's reasons for taking a particular stance on an issue and will aid in readers' evaluation of the author's ideas.

It is our hope that these books will give readers a deeper understanding of the issues debated and an appreciation of the complexity of even seemingly simple issues when good and honest people disagree. This awareness is particularly important in a democratic society such as ours in which people enter into public debate to determine the common good. Those with whom one disagrees should not be regarded as enemies but rather as people whose views deserve careful examination and may shed light on one's own.

Thomas Jefferson once said that "difference of opinion leads to inquiry, and inquiry to truth." Jefferson, a broadly educated man, argued that "if a nation expects to be ignorant and free . . . it expects what never was and never will be." As individuals and as a nation, it is imperative that we consider the opinions of others and examine them with skill and discernment. The Opposing Viewpoints Series is intended to help readers achieve this goal.

David L. Bender and Bruno Leone,
Founders

Introduction

> "Outsourcing was 10 years ago, where you'd say, 'Let's send some software generation overseas.' This is not the outsourcing we're doing today. This is just where I am going to get something done. Now you say, 'Hey, half my PhDs in my R-and-D department would rather live in Singapore, Taiwan or China because their hometown is there and they can go there and still work for my company.' This is the next evolution."
>
> —Mike Splinter, CEO of Applied Materials

> "Something is broken when far-right CEOs wreck our economy by shipping jobs overseas and get tax breaks for it while working people suffer unemployment, foreclosures and fading hopes for the future. Something is broken in America when corporations hide profits in offshore tax shelters while refusing to create jobs at home."
>
> —Richard L. Trumka, president of AFL-CIO

In early July 2012, President Barack Obama's campaign launched a hard-hitting attack on Republican candidate Mitt Romney in a controversial television ad, alleging that Bain Capital—the private equity firm established and run by the former Massachusetts governor—had offshored jobs to low-wage countries like India and China during his fifteen-year tenure with the company.

The ad also claimed that the Republican presidential candidate supported tax breaks for companies that ship jobs overseas, calling him an "outsourcer-in-chief." By contrast, President Obama was portrayed in the ad as someone who "believes in insourcing" and who "fought to save the US auto industry." According to the Romney campaign, the claims in the television ad were erroneous.

Shortly after the television ad aired, media reports revealed that the Obama campaign had used some of the information presented in a *Washington Post* article as the basis for the claims made in the ad—even though the article never stated that US jobs were transferred overseas during Romney's tenure (1984 to 1999) at Bain Capital. What the June 21, 2012, article did say, however, was that Romney was "actively involved" in running the private equity firm that "owned companies that were pioneers in the practice of shipping work from the United States to overseas call centers and factories making computer components." Information for the *Washington Post* article was gleaned from Securities and Exchange Commission filings for Bain Capital.

Romney's campaign demanded a retraction from the *Post*, but the newspaper denied the request. A subsequent *Washington Post* article that ran on July 2, 2012, pointed out that Romney and his campaign staff were demanding a retraction of the original story based on the Obama campaign's incorrect interpretation of the article, not on the actual facts presented in it. According to the follow-up article written by Glenn Kessler, the original story never said "that transfers of US jobs took place while Romney ran the private equity firm of Bain Capital. . . . Instead, the article says that Bain was prescient in identifying an emerging business trend—the movement of back-office, customer service, and other functions out of companies that were willing to let third parties handle that business. Several of the companies mentioned in the article grew into major international players in the offshoring field today."

Campaign ads, allegations, and political volleys aside, one nonpartisan, undisputed fact began to emerge during the 2012 presidential campaign: outsourcing was a hot-button issue.

President Obama had started beating the outsourcing drum months before the outsourcing television ads began airing. "My message is simple," Obama said during his January 2012 State of the Union address. "It's time to stop rewarding businesses that ship jobs overseas, and start rewarding companies that create jobs right here in America."

During that same speech, Obama also began outlining his "Blueprint for an America Built to Last." In it, Obama called for an end to tax incentives that encourage companies to send jobs overseas by requiring American companies to pay a minimum tax on overseas profits. Obama also called for a tax credit to help pay moving expenses for American companies that agreed to shut down overseas operations to bring jobs back to American soil as part of his "insourcing" agenda. His plan also included lowering tax rates for manufacturers, doubling tax deductions for high-tech manufacturers, issuing tax credits to companies making investments in regions hardest hit by job losses, stepping up trade enforcement, and providing financing to American companies facing competitors with unfair export financing.

For his part, Romney began talking tough about China, calling the Chinese "cheaters" and currency manipulators. Romney also started talking about his plans to impose large tariffs on Chinese exports if elected into office. In campaign ads, Romney vowed to "stand up to China."

Rhetoric from both presidential campaigns drew attention from China's largest newspaper, the *People's Daily*. The Communist Party newspaper published commentary denouncing both presidential campaigns in late June 2012. The newspaper said that the United States needed to focus on expanding production and encouraging consumer spending rather than railing against China. "Talking down on China and coming up with all sorts of trade protectionism is a cowardly way to avoid these problems," a commentator for the paper wrote. "Playing the 'China card' is not inspired, and cannot save the U.S. economy."

Regardless of party affiliation, the political rhetoric of the 2012 presidential campaign highlighted outsourcing as a critical issue, as well as the role it may have played in the challenging economic conditions that characterized President Obama's first term in office. And as the American public began to sift for the truth amid all the campaign promises and claims, disappointing numbers began to emerge about the state of the US economy only days after President Obama's first outsourcing ads began airing on television.

With the election only four months away, the June 2012 jobs report revealed that only eighty thousand jobs were created that month, resulting in an unemployment rate that remained unchanged at 8.2 percent. For investors and many others, the report fueled concerns about the US economy and its recovery from the recession. Romney and other Republicans also pointed to the June jobs report as further evidence that President Obama's economic policies were ineffective in reviving the US economy and delivering it from the damaging effects of a protracted recession. Upon hearing the June jobs report, Romney said in a July 6 news conference that the figures were a "kick in the gut for middle-class families," adding that President Obama's policies were to blame for continuing high unemployment. On the campaign trail in Ohio when the report was released, President Obama downplayed the disappointing news, pointing instead to the 4.4 million jobs created in the previous twenty-eight months following what he characterized as "the worst economic crisis of our lifetime." In an interview with an Ohio NBC television station, WLWT in Cincinnati, President Obama claimed other economic victories as well. "We saved an auto industry. That saved hundreds of thousands of jobs here in Ohio," he said.

In addition to criticism about the weak jobs report, some also criticized President Obama's record on outsourcing issues. Critics pointed out that he had promised to stem the flow of jobs overseas by reforming federal tax codes that made running overseas operations attractive to companies. Some maintained that President Obama had not made good on these campaign promises during his first term in office and that he should have done more to address outsourcing through reform of US trade policies, guest worker visa programs, and other policies.

As the presidential campaign wore on, millions of Americans weighed the candidates' position on outsourcing along with a wide range of other issues as they prepared to go to the polls in November. And against the backdrop of lingering economic woes and concerns about jobs, it was clear in the months leading up to the November election that the winner—regardless of political party affiliation—would have to address outsourcing and a number of other related issues after taking the oath of office in January 2013.

In *Opposing Viewpoints: Outsourcing*, writers debate a number of outsourcing-related issues, including its impact on the US economy, the global economy, on individual workers, and on corporations, through chapters titled, What Is the Global Impact of Outsourcing?, Is Outsourcing Good for Business?, What Impact Has Outsourcing Had on the US Economy?, and How Should the US Government Regulate Outsourcing? While the viewpoints vary widely in their scope and focus, the fact remains that we live in a global economy, and with the hyperconnectivity that technology and the Internet provide, geographic and international borders continue to blur more and more by the day.

OPPOSING
VIEWPOINTS®
SERIES

What Is the Global Impact of Outsourcing?

Chapter Preface

Peer into any café or walk down nearly any street in the United States, England, India, China, or countless other countries all over the globe, and you are likely to spot someone talking or texting on a cell phone, surfing the Internet, connecting to a social media site on a tablet PC, or sending a work e-mail from a laptop computer. The rapid advancement of technology has dramatically changed how people communicate with one another, how they collaborate on work projects, and how companies operate on a national and international scale. And increasingly, the hyperconnectivity that technology allows is effectively erasing the impact of traditional geographic borders on the global economy. With the lightning speed that technology allows, employees of a multinational company in the United States can immediately connect with their colleagues in Europe, Asia, or other parts of the world, thereby increasing efficiency, productivity, and the speed at which goods and services are made available to the global marketplace.

Today, more than 60 percent of the world's gross domestic product comes from global trade—double what it was in the 1980s, according to David Bornstein in the November 3, 2011, *New York Times* article, "Workers of the World, Employed." Many economists believe that the dramatic increase in international trade in the past twenty-five to thirty years has resulted in unprecedented economic growth, job creation, and reduction in poverty in many parts of the world. The integration of markets worldwide also has accelerated over the past several decades— due in part to fewer international trade barriers.

According to Michael Spence in "Globalization and Unemployment: The Downside of Integrating Markets," in the July–August 2011 issue of *Foreign Affairs*, an increasing number of developing countries have experienced sustained growth rates of 7 to 10 percent for twenty-five years or more. Income levels in many developing countries are approaching those in some of the more developed countries, and as a result, the impact of emerging economies on the global economy and the economies in more advanced countries is increasing. However, some also believe that globalization has resulted in the relocation of critical supply chains, negatively impacting employment, income levels, and the price of goods and services in advanced economies like the United States.

For all the criticism of globalization and outsourcing, however, there are those who point to the positive impact that outsourcing has had on people in the poorest regions of the world. Thanks to technological advances, some of these people now have the ability to tap the global marketplace and lift themselves and their entire communities out of poverty. Some of these opportunities come from organizations that practice what is known as impact sourcing, which involves outsourcing business processes or microtasks to people from impoverished or remote communities in developing countries. With the increasing cost of outsourcing as a whole, a number of organizations are drawn to impact sourcing because it generally utilizes workers who are less expensive to hire—generally due to their more remote locations and lower education levels. While some have expressed concern that this practice may lead to the creation of virtual sweatshops, others view it as a legitimate and socially responsible way to help lift people out of poverty while lowering the costs of doing business at the same time.

Authors of the viewpoints in this chapter debate the global impact of outsourcing from several different perspectives, highlighting the benefits and perils of increased globalization and outsourcing and how both continue to impact American and foreign workers, companies, and economies all over the world.

> "As a result of an increasing expected demand for IS [impact sourcing] services over the next five years, the client mix for IS is expected to shift slightly to a greater share of international work."

Offshore Outsourcing Helps Workers All Over the World

Monitor Company Group

The Monitor Company Group is a strategy consulting firm based in Cambridge, Massachusetts. In the following viewpoint, the group explores the growth of a practice called impact sourcing (IS), which the Monitor Company Group defines as the creation of sustainable jobs by business process outsourcing (BPO) firms for people living on annual incomes of less than $3,000. The Monitor Company Group estimates that IS will continue to grow over the next few years as companies continue to look for cost savings and greater efficiency through outsourcing. The group explains that the IS industry currently accounts for an estimated $4.5 billion in revenue. By 2015, the group maintains, it is estimated that the impact sourcing industry's market share could increase to $20 billion.

As you read, consider the following questions:

1. According to the author, how many people does the IS industry currently employ, and how many will the industry employ by the year 2015?
2. Who, according to the Monitor Company Group, are the primary impact sourcing clients?
3. What organizations does the author say tend to consider social responsibility rather than cost when selecting IS as an option?

Today [June 2011], the total global IS [impact sourcing] market generates an estimated $4.5 billion in revenues, representing 3.8 percent of the entire $119 billion BPO [business process outsourcing] industry and directly employing about 144,000 people across all segments. Of this, $1.2 billion is estimated to reach IS workers as employment income. Analysis suggests that the share of IS in total BPO could increase to approximately $20 billion in 2015, directly accounting for 780,000 jobs and just over 11 percent of the $178 billion total BPO market. Of this, more than $10 billion will reach IS workers through employment income.

The growth of IS can be seen as being driven by four key factors. First, there is the continuing expansion of the global demand for BPO services overall. Second, there is increased domestic demand for outsourcing in emerging economies (not just from the private, but also from the public sector, supported in particular by e-government and record digitization trends). Third, there are cost pressures that will push traditional BPO services into cheaper locations in peri-urban and rural areas. Fourth and finally, there are rising wage expectations among traditional BPO employees that will force service providers to open up lower-end tasks for less-educated individuals.

IS Expected to Grow

Analysis suggests that by the year 2015, direct IS employment in all segments could result in approximately 624,000 additional indirect jobs, which include all associated IS jobs such as managerial positions, with 3.2 million lives impacted. . . .

IS affects various populations in different ways, occurs across a broad range of contexts, and requires very specific interventions depending on the context.

For instance, IS occurs in low-employment parts of high-income countries when less-educated individuals receive BPO employment. IS also takes place in upper-middle-income countries with organizations employing individuals without tertiary [college] education. But here, different, specific interventions are required to grow the sector. For lower-income nations, the market size of IS varies significantly. Interventions necessary to bolster IS in places with an established BPO industry vary significantly across urban areas and rural regions.

On the other hand, countries without an established BPO industry need to engage in similar actions in urban and rural areas to push IS forward. Part of this requires establishing the viability of an overall BPO sector in the country. The exceptions here are interventions to strengthen IS for rural individuals who did not complete high school but who have attained basic literacy. Interventions for these workers would be largely similar in lower-income countries with or without an established BPO industry.

A Strong Business Case

Key components of the business case for IS focus mostly around the ability of ISSPs [impact sourcing service providers] to provide a high-quality service for a cost that is typically 40 percent lower than an average established urban BPO. This is especially compelling for the rural operators in India who are competing against an established set of players with contracts already in place. IS leverages the fact that for certain tasks, base-of-the-pyramid service providers cost less to employ and can undertake small-scale, sometimes part-time work that is often unattractive to traditional BPOs. However, three factors help determine the

Outsourcing Has Benefits

Social outsourcing has delivered sufficient benefits to warrant greater attention by other governments and by development agencies. . . .

Overall, social outsourcing shows how business and development can be brought together. Poverty reduction and empowerment are being achieved through social outsourcing not by rejecting business but by embracing it: by creating new enterprises; by seeking to create new entrepreneurs and by demonstrating how small business can deliver development goals.

Richard Heeks and Shoba Arun, Wiley InterScience, March 30, 2009.

competitiveness of an ISSP: (a) the comparative cost of recruiting IS employees, (b) the comparative cost of training these employees, and c) the comparative rate of employee attrition.

These comparative data highlight the fact that rural ISSPs in India benefit from lower salaries, lower training costs, lower attrition, and similar telecom costs to their urban counterparts. This combination of factors creates a cost advantage for the ISSPs, and also indicates what levers potential field builders can pull in addressing key challenges to help ensure that these organizations have compelling value for their customers.

There are countervailing costs [costs that need to be compensated for] to consider as well—especially for those managing rural BPOs. These costs include backup power and connectivity, plus the high cost and difficulty of attracting and retaining middle management. These cost constraints will emerge more significantly as the IS field begins to grow beyond the relatively limited number of centers in place currently.

Saving Money Drives IS

Current IS clients are private-sector companies, telecommunication firms, third-party BPO providers, and local and international organizations outsourcing segments of their business processes. On the public side, government constitutes a key client, especially through e-government services and archive digitization. Foundations and educational institutions are other public clients currently and potentially buying from ISSPs. . . .

Similar to conventional BPO customers, IS customers primarily desire cost savings and increased efficiency through outsourcing. Based on interviews, it appears that only a small proportion of IS clients are driven primarily by the desire to invest in a social cause. A substantial portion of potential clients for IS say they are interested in it primarily for cost savings. Their main interest is receiving a certain quality of services for the most competitive price, and with a minimum risk of failure. Buyers will then have a set of secondary criteria around language requirements, security needs, scale preferences and turnaround speed. An IS "label" may be seen as adding value—but only if the buyer's quality and price requirements are met first. Buyer interviews suggest that most clients know where the work is processed, but are initially hesitant to outsource to IS destinations if these are perceived to be less developed in terms of infrastructure, technology or education levels. Interviewees, however, expressed broad agreement that when such concerns are overcome, there is an interest in competitive IS services.

A much smaller segment of clients, whose mission may be socially oriented, would prefer ISSPs to traditional BPOs and could have a certain willingness to pay a premium for IS services. Universities, large NGOs [nongovernmental organizations] and charitable organizations fall into this category. Especially where such organizations fear public pushback for outsourcing some of their services, IS could present an effective and socially responsible alternative that could even be seen as enhancing their brand.

Increased International Focus

As a result of an increasing expected demand for IS services over the next five years [2011–2016], the client mix for IS is expected to shift slightly to a greater share of international work. Today, we estimate that international services account for 10 percent of all IS, a figure which is expected to rise to 25 percent by 2015.

Of the overall BPO market, basic voice services account for 30 percent, and basic data work 17 percent, which combined constitute almost all of what we believe to be the total addressable services market for IS. Within this addressable market, voice services for IS split into (a) basic inbound calls for domestic and international clients, and (b) in- and outbound voice for domestic clients. Within the "basic data services," experts expect the more low-value services (i.e., form data entry, transcription, image-tagging and digitization services) to be relevant for both international and domestic clients. Knowledge-based services, such as document publishing and management, as well as location-based knowledge services such as local research, are expected together to be more relevant for domestic clients.

The IS service mix is expected to shift from its current composition. Currently, data work constitutes an estimated 90 percent of IS with the remaining 10 percent of IS coming from voice services. Driven by an expected increased local demand in emerging markets, voice work is anticipated to increase to approximately 20 percent by 2015.

"By farming out production to suppliers in China and other low-wage countries with few labor protections, [US companies] often have outsourced not just work but worker."

Bad Apple: Could the Era of Exploitation Outsourcing Be Near Its End?

Ed Frauenheim

In the following viewpoint, Ed Frauenheim—a senior editor at Workforce Management—argues that reports of worker exploitation and poor working conditions at Apple Inc. are not unique to that company. He argues that consumers' lack of concern about how products are made and companies' search for cheap labor have led to worker abuse as these items often are made in regions with few labor protections. Nevertheless, Frauenheim notes that the trend toward worker exploitation appears to be shifting as consumers seem to be paying more attention to how workers are treated all along the supply chain—even as favorite products like iPhones and iPods are produced.

As you read, consider the following questions:
1. According to Frauenheim, what percentage of Americans mentioned Apple's overseas labor practices as a concern in late 2011?
2. An Apple executive quoted by the author says that customers care more about a new iPhone than what?
3. What is "less and less viable," and what is coming to a close, according to Frauenheim?

Recent scathing stories about working conditions in the creation of iPads and iPhones are a telling moment for Apple Inc. and other global corporations. Could this latest episode of outrage over worker mistreatment at an outsourced factory signal that the age of exploitation outsourcing is waning? I think so.

You've probably heard about one or both of the stories that have rattled Apple's massive customer base and the rest of the public. First, *This American Life* broadcast the first-person account of Mike Daisey, a self-proclaimed Apple enthusiast who traveled to China to see how Apple products were made—and was horrified at what he found.

Then the *New York Times* published a long story about harsh, dangerous working conditions at factories making Apple products. Daisey says he met with workers whose hand joints have "disintegrated" from repetitive work, while the *New York Times* piece centered on the tale of a young employee killed in an explosion of aluminum dust—not long after an advocacy group warned Apple of aluminum dust problems.

Apple is far from alone in tapping cheaper overseas labor employed by third-party firms. Many U.S. companies have tried to wash their hands of the actual making of things. They may have decent or enlightened labor practices for their direct employees. But by farming out production to suppliers in China and other low-wage countries with few labor protections, they often have outsourced not just work but worker abuse.

What Can Consumers Do About Worker Exploitation?

What can consumers do? They can buy competitive products (Samsung Galaxy . . . no Galaxy factories blew up last year), they can sign petitions, they can send emails (to Apple), or they can protest at stores. Each one of course has different impacts, and requires a different level of investment by the consumer, but each is available. That being said, for there to be a direct change in Apple, by Apple, there would need to be a real collective effort.

So far, even with all the press this has not happened.

Richard Brubaker, Asia Society,
March 1, 2012.

This is not a new story. In recent decades, the public has heard withering tales of clothing-makers such as Nike Inc. outsourcing to third-party firms that took advantage of workers in the developing world. Even in consumer electronics, substandard labor treatment in the supply chain has been proclaimed in the media since at least 2006. That's when a British publication reported harsh working conditions in the making of the iPod at Apple supplier Foxconn—the same company at the heart of the recent allegations.

But for the most part, U.S. consumers have been willing to turn a blind eye to Apple and others. A *New York Times* survey of Americans late last year found that only 2 percent mentioned Apple's overseas labor practices as a concern.

In essence, consumers have focused on Apple's remarkable products rather than how they are produced. That goes for me, too. I have written critically about labor issues at Apple. But I've had a series of Mac laptop computers for more than a decade. And as I compose this blog item, I'm listening to our family's iPod.

Apple has addressed supply-chain problems in recent years to some degree. But our collective apathy about working conditions behind iPods, iPhones and the like has allowed the company to prioritize speed and profit over decent treatment of people.

"You can either manufacture in comfortable, worker-friendly factories, or you can reinvent the product every year, and make it better and faster and cheaper, which requires factories that seem harsh by American standards," a current Apple executive told the *Times.* "And right now, customers care more about a new iPhone than working conditions in China."

But that's changing. In recent years, there has been a shift in attitudes among consumers toward a desire to do business with companies that show "kindness" in their operations. People also are increasingly identifying as "global citizens," meaning they have more empathy for people on the other side of the world. What's more, tools such as Facebook, Twitter and YouTube give people more opportunities to express themselves. This means companies increasingly face penalties for mistreating people— whether those workers are direct employees or not.

The *New York Times* story on iPad working conditions, for example, generated 1,770 reader comments. Many, if not most, blasted Apple or the overall system of cheap labor. And an online petition prompted by the *This American Life* piece that calls for Apple to protect Chinese workers has garnered roughly 166,000 signatures—and counting.

"We care about every worker in our worldwide supply chain," Apple CEO Tim Cook reportedly wrote in a memo to employees in the wake of the stories. But the public isn't buying it. It sees some rotten labor practices at the core of Apple. And, increasingly, people, including Apple's own employees, will demand better of the company.

The bottom line for Apple and other companies is that a shameful supply chain is less and less viable. Happily, the age of farming out worker exploitation is coming to a close.

> *"Our mission is to eliminate poverty [through outsourcing jobs]. To do that effectively, poor people need to directly increase their income in a measurable way."*

Socially Responsible Outsourcing Can Reduce Poverty Worldwide

Leila Janah, as told to Christina Hernandez Sherwood

Leila Janah is founder and CEO of the San Francisco–based non-profit Samasource. In the following viewpoint, she discusses how her organization uses the outsourcing of micro-tasks through contracts with companies like Google and LinkedIn to supply work to some of the poorest people in the world. By providing work to people in countries like India, Uganda, and Haiti, Janah hopes to eliminate poverty and boost local economies by providing sustainable jobs and opportunities for small-scale entrepreneurs. As Janah points out, outsourcing in this way is not harming workers in the United States because the work consists of "bottom of the rung" tasks that do not leverage the skill sets of American workers.

As you read, consider the following questions:

1. What is the biggest impediment to economic growth in poor countries, according to Janah?
2. According to the author, why are the micro-tasks that Samasource workers perform not taking jobs away from American workers?
3. How does Samasource break down projects into micro-tasks for workers in impoverished countries, according to Janah?

Christina Hernandez Sherwood: Talk about the Samasource mission.
Leila Janah: We take data contracts from companies like Google and LinkedIn and Ask.com. We have technology systems that break down that work into micro-tasks that anybody who has a bit of training and access to a computer and the Internet can do. We farm out those micro-tasks to some of the poorest people in the world—in parts of Kenya and India and Haiti, in Pakistan and Uganda. The people who do the work are working from local partner centers. These are partner organizations, about 50 percent nonprofit and 50 percent for-profit, that all have in common a social mission. They maintain computers and Internet access. The partners allow us to add more workers without adding a lot of administrative overhead. We have 16 partners and we've dispersed more than $600,000 to workers.

Our mission is to eliminate poverty. To do that effectively, poor people need to directly increase their income in a measurable way—not through the trickle-down effect. In parallel, we need to build up the capacity of small-scale entrepreneurs who can start up businesses and get the wheels of the economy turning. The biggest impediment to economic growth in poor countries is that the bottom layer of entrepreneurs—those who own mom and pop shops and corner stores—needs to get plugged more directly into the global economy.

Lower-Level Entrepreneurs

Samasource takes lower level entrepreneurs and gives them access to a business model that plugs them directly into the supply chains of large technology enterprises in the U.S. and Europe. That facilitates a direct flow of wealth from rich countries to poor countries, but in reward for work as opposed to handouts. That happened previously, but through many, many layers of middlemen. We've facilitated a direct engagement between a small-scale entrepreneur in a place like Kenya and a company like LinkedIn.

Who are the workers?

There's a young man in Kenya named Steve Muthee who I met in 2008. He'd graduated from college in Kenya, but the country had high unemployment. He decided to become an entrepreneur. He took out a loan, got four computers and started digitizing old court records. He hired university students. They were using the money to fund their education. When I met Steve, he had these four computers in a tiny corner of the central business district in Nairobi. It was a really decrepit space. Steve said, If you could find me the contracts, I could grow this business. I came back here, started Samasource and found our very first contract digitizing books.

Steve has grown his business from four people to more than 50 people in a year and a half. Some of his workers have the most inspiring stories. I met a young guy named Benson who can get a college degree because he spends four hours a day doing this digitization work. Samasource gives people not only work, but this sense of dignity that comes from being part of the new economy. We've helped more than 900 workers like Benson and more than 25 entrepreneurs like Steve.

Economic Opportunities for the Poor

How much money are people making from Samasource work?

It varies a lot by region. We commit to paying a living wage. We determine our wages through the Fair Wage Guide. Our part-

Samasource Worker Profile

- *Average age*: 24 years
- *Education*: 70% university graduates, 30% high school graduates
- *Male: Female ratio*: 50:50
- *Background*: In Kenya most employees are urban (lower) middle class, in India workers have less education and are often rural
- *Compensation [per month]*: Earn $80–$280—majority of peers are unemployed and dependent on their families
- *Attrition*: Varies depending on service providers from negligible amounts to nearly 30%

Monitor Group, "Job Creation Through Building the Field of Impact Sourcing," June 2011.

ners are required to report wages of workers and we make sure they're above that floor. Generally, that's not a problem because this work is so much higher paid than anything they could be doing locally. Artisan craft makers are making 50 cents an hour in many cases. With Samasource they're able to make, at the base level, 70 cents to $1 an hour in parts of India. In parts of Kenya, they're able to make several dollars an hour.

But getting fixated on dollar amounts is problematic. That work would never get done here. It hasn't been done here for a long time. It's just hard to compare. People don't understand what $1 or $2 means in terms of purchasing power where our workers live. We've faced some backlash because there's a perception that we're taking jobs away from America, but it's just not accurate.

How so?

When I buy a fair trade handbag made by artisans in rural India through a job creation program for women, I don't think: I'm outsourcing the production of this handbag to Indian people. I think: I'm providing economic opportunity for someone who is poor. But because of the nature of digital work, there's a perception that it should be going to people in wealthier countries or it is work that is ours as Americans. That perception needs to shift.

We're doing the most basic tasks within the outsourcing space. We're doing the bottom rung of the work that even the big outsourcing firms in India and China and the Philippines don't want to do because the margin is pretty low. This basic task completion is so routine, it doesn't leverage the skill set of a person educated in America. When we think about rebuilding the American economy, the pillars of that growth need to leverage the education level of Americans, which is substantially above the education level of someone in rural India or rural Africa.

Samasource Is Expanding

How does Samasource use technology?

Our main technology is a web software tool we've built that breaks down data projects into micro-tasks and then allocates those micro-tasks to workers. It allows entrepreneurs like Steve to manage their centers through our technology. Steve is able to pull down tasks for his work team. All the workers at his center log in and do work and Steve can manage the quality on his own. Our managers here in San Francisco do quality assurance on the work once it has been done by his workers. As the workers do tasks, they earn points. The points translate into payments.

We're experimenting with giving workers educational tasks. They do 50 basic data entry tasks, then as a break they'll watch a TED [technology, entertainment, and design] Talk or do a short

English-language quiz or do another educational task. Over two years, they could get a good knowledge of a particular subject. It's important to make this rote work more interesting and more beneficial for our workers.

What's next for Samasource?

The big question for us right now is how we take this model to scale—how we move from the workers we help now to many more workers in the future. Our goal is to hit 10,000 by 2012, which is a really ambitious goal. To do that, we need to figure out how we can replicate the partner models. How do we create more Steves? How do we standardize the business format, so we can adopt lots of them in one place and have them start a center off of the Samasource platform?

This year, we're going to launch a lab in Kenya—our first experiment at replicating a business like Steve's in our own way. We're doing all sorts of things to reduce the cost of the center. That's going to be our standard business format that we replicate —almost like a franchise—across one geography to start.

| "*Outsourcing is thriving and will only get bigger—both in India and other foreign shores, but right here in the U.S. as well.*"

Outsourcing to US Workers Is a Growing Trend with Economic Advantages

Vivek Wadhwa

Vivek Wadhwa is a technology entrepreneur and academic who is also vice president of academics and innovation at Singularity University in Silicon Valley, California. In the following viewpoint, Wadhwa says that while many view outsourcing as a negative for US workers, the practice is actually creating jobs all over the United States through companies like oDesk, which supplies temporary skilled workers to businesses in need of technology, database design, and other services. The author also points out that there are a number of foreign companies that routinely outsource to US workers. Outsourcing is thriving, Wadhwa says, and it likely will continue growing overseas as well as on American soil.

As you read, consider the following questions:

1. According to Wadhwa, what are some of the factors that have led to an increase in outsourcing in the United States and in other parts of the world?

2. According to the author's research, what are some of the countries that are outsourcing to American workers?

3. How can "smallsourcing" help US workers in rural areas, according to Wadhwa?

Outsourcing is a dirty word. In the U.S., outsourcing means firing full-time workers and shipping their jobs to a less developed country where wages are lower and labor laws are more lax. With U.S. unemployment closing in on 10%, and estimates of real unemployment (including part-time workers) climbing to over 15%, the idea of cutting American jobs and shipping them abroad is morally offensive to many.

So imagine my surprise when I found out that one small corner of the outsourcing business was going great guns—and that one of the fastest-growing destinations for outsourced jobs is none other than the U.S.

Online Contracting Grows

I came to this conclusion after reviewing the statistics of oDesk, one of several companies that connect people in need of skilled temporary work with employees who fit the bill. ODesk provides the infrastructure to make it easier to monitor, manage, and pay consultants working in remote locations. The number of hours worked on oDesk projects by contractors has risen threefold over the past 12 months. The rise of oDesk and competitors such as eLance illustrate how the world has become not only a freelance economy but also, by extension, an outsourced economy.

This outcome is driven by several key factors. First, the Internet makes it easier to assemble and manage remote teams of workers. Second, increasing economic pressures in the global economy spurred by the rise of the developing world as a global competitor have forced all firms to eliminate some full-time positions, and instead rely more on contractors.

"Rural Sourcing" vs. Offshoring

The concept of "rural sourcing," whereby U.S.–based service providers establish delivery centers in low-cost regions outside of major metropolitan areas, is gaining increasing interest and credibility as a viable alternative to global offshoring.

Potential benefits include access to relatively low-cost labor, fewer time-zone and cultural constraints, and, in many cases, lower transition costs. For many organizations, especially those in the public sector, the political appeal of maintaining domestic operations can be paramount.

Kathy Welch, Information Services Group, 2012.

Last, many small and midsize businesses now regularly need real technology help, whether it's to build Web sites and databases, craft user interfaces, or install software. They also need help to babysit and develop this technology. Small businesses were the least well-equipped and are the most under-resourced. So naturally they turned to the new global freelance market, at first for technology skills and then for help in marketing, accounting, and other areas.

"Smallsourcing" Thrives Despite Predictions

Some predicted that freelancing would wither under the financial crisis as firms cut spending for IT [information technology] development work. But that clearly hasn't happened, if the numbers from oDesk are to be believed. Contractors offer a wide variety of skills, ranging from data entry to sophisticated computer programming. Customers vary from small businesses and sole proprietors seeking project help to large businesses that don't have internal skills for a certain type of job.

What's perhaps the most interesting facet of this new brand of outsourcing—which I call "smallsourcing"—is the truly global nature of the workforce and the work being outsourced. ODesk has contractors from dozens of countries, including China, Singapore, Russia, and Bolivia. At the same time, work is being outsourced to the U.S. from the United Kingdom, Canada, Australia, Spain—even Saudi Arabia and the United Arab Emirates. While the single largest percentage of oDesk work goes to contractors in India, the U.S. ranks No. 3. And the number of hours worked in the U.S. is growing at a pace of 267%, considerably faster than the 188% for India.

The salary differentials between India and the U.S. are far smaller than one might have thought, according to oDesk billing data. Indian workers were paid roughly $11 an hour on average and U.S. workers were paid roughly $17.50 an hour. But Americans receive higher evaluations for their work—an average 4.48 out of 5, compared with 4.12 for India. So the Americans don't have that much of a disadvantage. Companies readily pay a little more for higher-quality work.

"Smallsourcing" Gives Employers Flexibility

True, smallsourcing pits workers in high-wage countries against those in low-wage countries. That will necessarily mean downward pressures on wages in developed countries for freelancers in specialties where foreign freelancers can easily compete. But smallsourcing could help raise the bar in locations such as rural parts of the U.S. In many of those places a $17.50-an-hour job is considered very solid and real estate prices are low enough to allow someone to buy a house with this level of take-home pay. Plus, highly skilled workers can make much more. Some with Web design and system administration skills earn $60 to $90 an hour.

As health-care expenses continue to rise and the costs of full-time employment grow in tandem, outsourcing inevitably will increase. Building a variable-cost labor structure is a necessity for many employers who need the flexibility to pay higher rates when the economy is good and lower rates when the economy is bad.

For the project workers who log in to oDesk every day to create their own job with decent pay, outsourcing is a wonderful thing—be it in Wyoming or New Delhi. Some have been forced from full-time jobs but many simply prefer to go it alone or to work with small groups. Scarred by a barrage of layoffs in recent years, these workers like the control over their lives and diversity in the source of paychecks.

In a world of uncertainty, one thing is certain: Outsourcing is thriving and will only get bigger—both in India and other foreign shores, but right here in the U.S. as well.

Periodical and Internet Sources Bibliography

The following articles have been chosen to supplement the diverse views presented in this chapter.

Bruce Einhorn	"The Philippines Astounds the Skeptics," *Bloomberg Businessweek*, May 3, 2012.
Thomas L. Friedman	"Made in the World," *New York Times*, January 28, 2012.
John Helyar	"Outsourcing: A Passage Out of India," *Bloomberg Businessweek*, March 15, 2012.
Frank Holmes	"Your Next Call to Tech Support May Be Answered in the Philippines," *Business Insider*, April 23, 2012. www.businessinsider.com.
Saritha Rai	"How Outsourcing Is Boosting Prospects for Indian Women," CNET, May 5, 2012. http://news.cnet.com.
Seema Sirohi	"How 'Outsourcing' Taints India's Contribution to US," *Firstpost*, April 30, 2012. www.firstpost.com.
V. Sridhar	"Is the Outsourcing Story Unravelling?," *Hindu* (Chennai, India), April 29, 2012. www.thehindu.com.
Jo Washington	"City Governments Turn to Samasource, Crowd4all, and Crowdflower to Help Fight Poverty," *PolicyMic*, January 31, 2012. www.policymic.com.
Chen Xin	"Outsourced Workers Call for Change," *China Daily*, May 7, 2012. www.chinadaily.com.
Chi-Chi Zhang	"Apple Manufacturing Plant Workers Complain of Long Hours, Militant Culture," CNN, February 6, 2012. www.cnn.com.

Is Outsourcing Good for Business?

Chapter Preface

For many companies, outsourcing is viewed as a way to lower costs, boost efficiency, and free up time and resources to focus on core business activities. To accomplish this, an increasing number of companies are hiring business process outsourcing (BPO) firms to handle front- and back-office business functions like human resources, finance, accounting, customer care, and information technology.

Many multinational companies employ BPO firms located overseas in locations like India and the Philippines. But the Dow Chemical Company took a different approach in 2011 when it partnered with India-based Tata Consultancy Services (TCS) and opened its primary Business Process Services Center in Midland, Michigan. Dow Chemical, a multinational chemical corporation, also has five other business service centers worldwide. The center in Midland, Michigan, provides finance, supply chain, human resources, information technology, and procurement services to the company. And instead of shipping the work overseas, Dow officials hired people from the surrounding region to fill many of the open positions. Company officials said contributing to the region's economic revival played a role in their decision to locate the business processing center at its world headquarters in Midland.

In other parts of the world, BPO firms are contributing to economic growth on a much larger scale. For example, according to a June 2012 article in the *Economist*, the BPO sector in the Philippines employs 638,000 people and brings in revenues of $11 billion, about 5 percent of that country's gross domestic product (GDP). Officials in that country estimate that the BPO industry has the potential to add another 700,000 jobs to the sector by 2016, as well as $25 billion in revenue—essentially one-tenth of that country's GDP.

Despite the boon to foreign economies and those who tout the benefits of BPOs and outsourcing in general, critics point out that the practice does not always result in cost savings and increased efficiency. In fact, a number of case studies in recent years highlight that outsourcing can lead to significant cost overruns. A 2012 survey of 250 information technology professionals that was conducted by Los Angeles–based Lieberman Software revealed that outsourcing sometimes results in higher-than-anticipated project costs. According to 42 percent of those polled, the cost of outsourcing agreements was higher than originally planned. And while many believe that outsourcing can help companies address a number of business challenges, others point out that outsourcing—when it goes awry—can create problems that are very costly and time-consuming to fix.

Others maintain that while outsourcing can help a company achieve cost savings in the short run, it can harm a company's long-term viability and profitability by destroying its ability to perform core business functions. Some also assert that outsourcing can damage a company's ability to perform research, development, and innovation activities—all the things that help assure a corporation's long-term viability and ability to compete in the global marketplace. Yet there are others who contend that outsourcing can actually lead to an increase in innovation since companies have the ability to tap a larger talent pool from all over the globe.

Regardless of their differing opinions on outsourcing, however, the writers of the viewpoints in this chapter seem to agree that companies are primarily motivated by the cost-savings potential of outsourcing. But as many examples in the viewpoints highlight, the success of the practice is largely dependent on the effectiveness of the company's overall strategy and the oversight it establishes to guide the outsourcing process. The authors explore the pros and cons of outsourcing as a short- and long-term business strategy, as well as the broader impact it has on American workers and the US economy.

| *"Companies clearly recognise the need to look outside their organisations for new sources of innovation."*

Outsourcing Can Boost Corporate Innovation

Sarah Murray

A *regular contributor to the* Financial Times *and other publications, writer Sarah Murray explores the findings of a study conducted by* The Economist *Intelligence Unit that outlines the growing trend of outsourcing innovation. In the report, Murray points out that many companies—faced with increasing market pressures and a shortage of talent and skilled labor—have found that outsourcing innovation is a way to save money and secure a competitive advantage in the global marketplace. Despite these benefits, however, some companies are reluctant to outsource innovation to third parties due to concerns about loss of intellectual property, but Murray points out that technological advances and other measures can help minimize these risks.*

As you read, consider the following questions:

1. According to the study cited by Murray, how much innovation came from external sources during the period surveyed?

2. Based on the study cited by the author, what percentage of companies believe that innovation will increasingly come from external sources?

3. According to information cited by Murray, what are some specific methods that companies can use to protect data and intellectual property?

A few decades ago, when companies thought of innovation, it was with a view to improving a product over a period of years. In-house R&D [research and development] teams would apply what they had learned and gradually adapt products to meet new requirements. Today, that process takes mere months.

As product lifecycles become more compressed and the complexity of the product development process escalates, companies are looking to broaden their supply of new ideas. As a result, they are turning to R&D capabilities that lie outside their organisations and embrace a variety of "open innovation" models. In the survey, 37% of respondents report that about one-quarter of the innovation emerging from their organisation in the past three years [2004–2007] came from external partners.

As well as the need to speed up the time in which they bring new products to market, the shortage of skills in mature markets—particularly in fields such as engineering and chemistry—is driving the need to look for new pools of talent in countries such as China and India. Our findings confirm this trend, with 39% of respondents saying that, in the past three years, it has become "somewhat harder" to hire talented employees who can deliver innovative ideas, with a further 19% seeing this as "much harder."

Benefits and Risks

However, the survey suggests that while most companies have a positive view of outsourced or open approaches to innovation and expect to obtain more ideas from external sources in the next three years, many have yet to do so. The largest group of respondents (41%) say that in the past three years their organisation derived little or no innovation from external partners. Only 13% report that about one-half of their innovation came from these sources.

Lack of trust appears to be a major obstacle to the willingness of companies to embrace the idea of turning innovation over to third parties. This was cited by 31% of respondents as the biggest barrier to the outsourcing of innovation, with 20% citing poor communications with external partners. Almost one-half (49%) of respondents see loss of intellectual property to competitors and business partners as the main risk in outsourcing innovation to partners.

However, companies clearly recognise the importance of external sources of innovation, with 29% of respondents seeing overall competitive advantage as the main benefit and 26% citing greater speed in getting products to market. The question for companies then is how they can capitalise on the benefits of sourcing innovation externally without losing their most valuable asset: their intellectual property.

The concept of open innovation has attracted the attention of many companies and academics in recent years. Henry Chesbrough, a business professor at the University of California, Berkeley, and author of *Open Innovation* and *Open Business Models*, argues that managers can tap into a vast pool of knowledge and ideas, many of which lie outside their organisations. Companies, he says, do not have to originate research in order to profit from it.

This is something that Procter & Gamble [P&G] has demonstrated. Over the past decade, the company has radically altered the way it sourced new ideas and products, using the Internet and other methods to turn to independent investors, universities and suppliers.

Companies have long recognised that they cannot do everything themselves. The whole outsourcing movement, now decades old, is based on the idea of handing over tasks such as manufacturing to third parties to allow a company to focus on what it does best, whether marketing, branding and selling or managing customer relationships.

A Growing Trend

But while outsourcing and offshoring were used purely as cost-cutting strategies, some organisations are looking to gain more from their relationships with external partners by tapping into their ability to innovate. This kind of strategy is seen as a good thing. In this survey, the biggest group of respondents (57%) believe that the proportion of innovation derived from external partners will increase in the next three years.

Respondents highlighted a range of benefits from deriving more innovation from external partners. The largest group see this as enhancing their organisation's R&D capabilities (53%), while 38% cite product and service development and 35% point to process efficiency.

Part of the driver behind the desire to increase use of external sources of innovation is the pressure to speed up product development cycles. In our research, 26% of respondents believe that deriving innovation from partners would help them get their products to market faster.

"By and large everything goes much faster these days," says Steven Veldhoen, a vice-president in Booz Allen Hamilton's Tokyo office and author of *Innovation: Is Global the Way Forward?*, a joint study by Booz Allen Hamilton and Insead. "I do a lot of work with automotive companies and the development cycles are shortening all the time."

Open Innovation Strategies

At the same time, the pipeline of talent needed to research and develop the innovations behind new products is shrinking in mature markets. Some 39% of respondents report that in the past three years it has become "somewhat harder" to recruit the kind of skilled workers needed to deliver innovative ideas, with 19% saying that this has become "much harder".

Growth in emerging markets is not helping, notes Ian Brinkley, Knowledge Economy programme director at the UK's Work Foundation. Mr Brinkley argues that, while companies once filled gaps with highly talented Asian engineers and scientists—many of whom stayed on after studying in the US or Europe—this may become harder.

"If the quality of educational institutions in Asia goes up and their own high-tech industries develop, creating more jobs, the future supply of high-quality labour coming into Western economies is going to slow dramatically," he says. "And this could potentially cause real problems."

Open innovation strategies may fill this talent gap. Procter & Gamble, for one, believes its open approach to sourcing innovation allows it to tap into vast pools of skilled individuals. "We have about 9,000 researchers internally, but if you look at the domain space those people play in and the number of researchers who are out there in the world as a whole, there are 1.5m [million] researchers in that space," says Bill Metz, the company's global business services external business development manager. "So anything we can to do to tap into them expands our capacity to innovate."

A Variety of Models

While there is much discussion about the need to take a more open approach to innovation, the models being deployed by companies vary dramatically, from the totally open approach, whereby companies solicit ideas from everyone from suppliers to customers, to the "captive site" model in which companies establish and operate their own R&D centres overseas.

Procter & Gamble's version of open innovation involves accessing externally developed intellectual property, assets and know-how and, once it has identified a property, a trademark, a service or a capability, doing a business transaction with its owner. "One of the challenges we face as we get bigger is that it's more and more difficult to grow organically through only your own internal R&D," says Mr Metz. "So we're turning to the outside to augment the capability that we have internally."

One of the ways P&G does this is through its connect+develop website, where individuals or companies can respond to the needs the company has posted or submit unsolicited input. The task then is for P&G to identify viable submissions to which the individuals offering them have the rights.

Other examples of open innovation include InnoCentive, an open innovation company that uses a website to offer financial rewards to people who solve specific criteria posted on the site, and Lego Factory, which allows the children that are Lego's customers to design products.

Our findings suggest that tapping into open sources of innovation in this way is something companies aspire to, with a large segment of respondents (59%) seeing an increase in the use of open sources of innovation at their organisation in the next three years.

Although the concept of "open innovation" has attracted much attention, Tim Jones, principal of Innovaro, a UK-based consultancy, argues that confusion often surrounds the term "open", and that the models are quite distinct from one another. "Open source is free of intellectual property [IP] and that's the whole point of it," he says. "Open innovation is all about trading intellectual property. If there's no IP, then you can't do the deal."

Sharing the Best Ideas

For many companies, however, externalising innovation means turning to existing suppliers and other business partners. "I see it happening pretty much everywhere," says Mr Veldhoen. "It's working with suppliers, getting best ideas from suppliers and working in a way that it's not just about delivering, but is also about sharing the best ideas."

Mr Brinkley identifies an additional version of external innovation. "Some of the models are simply joint funding or joint

Outsourcing Innovation Can Help Different Aspects of an Organization's Business

"What parts of your organization's business do you think would benefit most from outsourcing innovation and ideas? Select up to three."
(% respondents)

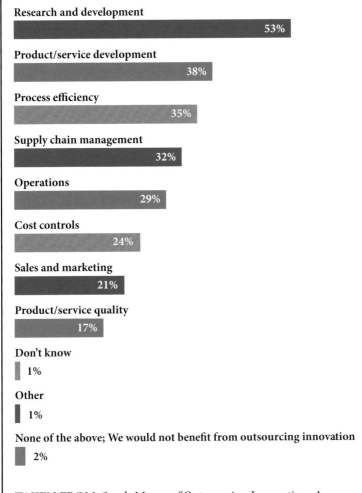

Research and development
53%

Product/service development
38%

Process efficiency
35%

Supply chain management
32%

Operations
29%

Cost controls
24%

Sales and marketing
21%

Product/service quality
17%

Don't know
1%

Other
1%

None of the above; We would not benefit from outsourcing innovation
2%

TAKEN FROM: Sarah Murray, "Outsourcing Innovation: A Manufacturer's Perspective," *The Economist* Intelligence Unit Report, sponsored by Siemens PLM Software, May 2008.

ventures, particularly in areas such as aerospace and pharmaceuticals. So the recent Rolls-Royce investments in Germany is effectively with the state government—it's not entirely a Rolls-Royce facility."

Often, it is users, rather than manufacturers, who are from necessity the innovators. Eric von Hippel, a professor at MIT Sloan School of Management and author of *Democratizing Innovation*, cites the example of Massachusetts General Hospital, which developed a slow-acting syringe that releases a small amount of fluid containing antibiotics into the bloodstream. This innovation would replace more expensive intravenous fluid bags and be better for patients. "They designed and tested the syringe before calling in manufacturers," he explains. "So the users are designing and testing the product—they are the true innovators in such cases."

Few Companies Are Outsourcing Innovation

With companies such as P&G, Boeing, GE [General Electric] and Dell continuing to capture headlines for their open approaches to sourcing innovation, many companies aspire to similar models. As the survey indicates, most companies expect the proportion of innovation derived from either external partners or open sources to increase. However, when polled on how much innovation has been derived from these sources over the past three years, the results are quite different.

Some 41% of respondents say that little or none of their innovation has been derived from external sources in the past three years, while only a tiny minority (2%) say that nearly all their innovation was externally sourced. More than one-half of respondents (54%) say that their organisation solicited innovation and ideas on an open-source basis only to a small extent, whereas a large proportion (51%) agree that their organisation was most successful at sourcing innovation in-house.

Part of the reason behind this mismatch between stated intent and actual activity may lie in the way companies define innovation—by the volume of new products and businesses they launch. The majority of companies in our survey (64%) measure innovation this way. The second most popular method, cited by 54% or respondents, is to tally the revenue growth from these launches, whereas 32% cite counting the number of patents filed as the method they used.

Yet such methods of accounting for innovation may leave out other types of innovation and process improvements that occur at the hands of external partners. "When you look at automotive companies such as BMW, GM or Toyota, they do open innovation all the time—it's just that they haven't called it that," says Mr Veldhoen. "So there could be a mis-definition of terms."

Lack of Trust Is a Barrier

However, a very real barrier to open approaches to innovation lies in many companies' lack of trust in their suppliers. As a result, companies worry that they could lose control of their intellectual property. Respondents to our survey cite this as the greatest danger posed by a strategy of deriving more innovation and ideas from external partners, with 25% citing the potential loss of IP to competitors and 24% citing loss of IP to partners.

These fears have been realised in some instances where contract manufacturers have made the leap from supplier to brand owner, as Acer, a computer manufacturer, has done. "Particularly in the computer world, you're getting these weird-sounding brands you've never heard of suddenly being available directly," says Mr Jones. "Those companies have grown by learning from the likes of Compaq and Dell, for whom they've been making products for years."

Worries over loss of intellectual property are heightened when it comes to operating in certain countries. "The big problem is China, where respect for intellectual property is less rigorous than elsewhere," confirms Mr Brinkley. "And you can never count on national jurisdictions enforcing the laws the way they ought to."

Protecting Intellectual Property

However, technology can be a powerful tool when it comes to protecting intellectual property. As companies increasingly hook suppliers into their networks to facilitate collaboration, it is crucial for them to monitor and control the information that is accessible via these networks. Options range from use of smart passwords to enterprise rights management software, which allows organisations to limit the data individuals can access and to control what those individuals can do with the data.

Almost half (49%) of respondents said their organisations deployed passwords and encryption when working with partners, while 33% said they used systems and project areas protected by firewalls. Enterprise rights management software was also used in the organisations of 26% of respondents. . . .

Faced with talent shortages and the need to speed up the time it takes to get new products on the market, companies clearly recognise the need to look outside their organisations for new sources of innovation. These sources can range from web-based communities of consumers and customers to universities, business partners and manufacturing suppliers.

However, our study shows that although companies acknowledge a need and intention to look externally for new ideas, evidence of activity in this area is weaker, with many respondents reporting that in the past three years little of their innovation has been derived from external partners or from organisations or individuals outside their network of suppliers.

In part, this may be because companies' definition of innovation—based on the number of products launched—means that they are not taking account of other innovations in the manufacturing process already taking place. However, the biggest barrier to outsourcing innovation is the fear of loss of intellectual property.

While this is a very real concern, companies that put in place contractual arrangements, robust collaborative project systems and efficient communication channels can minimise the risk of others capitalising on their ideas. In addition, growing availability of everything from data encryption systems to enterprise rights management software means companies can shore up protection of their most valuable intellectual assets.

And savvy companies have recognised that if they can strike the right balance between protecting these intellectual property assets and giving outsource partners sufficient access to information about their products and processes, those outsource partners can provide not just cost savings and flexibility, but also the ideas and innovations that, in a business environment moving ever faster, will help them continue to secure competitive advantage.

> *"As U.S. companies were steadily*
> *outsourcing development and*
> *manufacturing work abroad and*
> *cutting spending on basic research,*
> *American competitiveness and*
> *innovation eroded."*

IT Outsourcing: How Offshoring Can Kill Innovation

Willy Shih and Gary Pisano, as told to
Stephanie Overby

Willy Shih is a professor of management practice, and Gary Pi-
sano is the Harry Figgie Jr. Professor of Business Administration at
Harvard Business School. Stephanie Overby, a regular contributor
to CIO, *has also written for the* Christian Science Monitor, *the*
New York Times, and other publications. In the following view-
point, Overby interviews Shih and Pisano about how outsourcing
can have a negative, irreversible impact on a company's ability
to innovate and maintain a competitive advantage in the global
marketplace. The professors argue that companies can become too
reliant on third-party suppliers so that they are no longer able to
manufacture or develop product designs in-house. While outsourc-

ing often makes sense from a cost and skilled labor standpoint, the professors stress that companies must take steps to avoid damaging the long-term viability of their business operations.

As you read, consider the following questions:

1. According to Shih, what were the factors that damaged Kodak's business?
2. What advice do the professors offer to professionals in the IT field?
3. A company should never outsource what, according to the viewpoint?

CIO.com: You assert that as U.S. companies were steadily out-sourcing development and manufacturing work abroad and cutting spending on basic research, American competitiveness and innovation eroded. What's the most conclusive evidence of that?

Willy Shih, Professor of Management Practice, Harvard Business School: The troubling thing that our research turned up is that offshoring can lead to damage to what we call the industrial commons—a set of capabilities embodied in your supplier network, your workforce, the educational infrastructure associated with a technology area. For example, in the 1960s Kodak gave up making sophisticated film cameras, and the U.S. consumer electronics companies offshored their product manufacturing and development. So the industrial commons for consumer electronic and optoelectronic devices in the U.S. withered away. So when the digital camera revolution came along—even though Kodak invented the first digital camera in the 1970s—there was no longer any capability base in the U.S. to develop or manufacture such products.

Gary Pisano, Harry E. Figgie, Jr., Professor of Business Administration, Harvard Business School: Just look at what has happened in the mobile communications industry today. A lot of

PC companies first gave up manufacturing, and then design. They became reliant on third party suppliers. Now we see what Apple has done with the iPad, and it seems to me there are an awful lot of PC manufacturers scrambling to find an "off-the-shelf" design to compete in the tablet computing space. The problem is, from my perspective, there is nothing unique about any of those designs. They have not competed well against the iPad.

CIO.com: Proponents of offshore outsourcing say it not only cuts costs, but also can enable companies to focus on their core value. But you found that many companies developed a taste for offshore labor arbitrage and outsourced more high-value tasks. Why didn't they funnel offshore savings into innovation?

Shih: If outsourcing improves your numbers over the short term, sometimes it is difficult to take those savings and reinvest them. That was one of the drivers behind improving the numbers in the first place—bringing more to the bottom line. This is driven by the pursuit of profit, which is a good thing. I'm not being critical of that. But it highlights the importance of being thoughtful about outsourcing capabilities or damaging the commons.

Pisano: This is partly about having too short of a time perspective, but there is also something deeper. It's rooted in how many management teams have come to view their source of advantage. For many, it seems, the name of the game is arbitrage. The key is to be a good "trader." You find good opportunities to buy stuff less than you can do it yourself, and you capture the value on your brand. They do not see having unique capabilities as the true source of competitive advantage.

CIO.com: Many CIOs have also embraced offshoring and are moving more complex and higher-value tasks abroad. What can they take away from your research?

A Negative Impact on Innovation

The decline of manufacturing in a region sets off a chain reaction. Once manufacturing is outsourced, process-engineering expertise can't be maintained, since it depends on daily interactions with manufacturing. Without process-engineering capabilities, companies find it increasingly difficult to conduct advanced research on next-generation process technologies. Without the ability to develop such new processes, they find they can no longer develop new products. In the long term, then, an economy that lacks an infrastructure for advanced process engineering and manufacturing will lose its ability to innovate.

Gary Pisano and Willy Shih, Harvard Business Review, *July–August 2009.*

Shih: It is a cautionary tale about the importance of understanding the long-term capability strategy in your company and understanding where the needs for capabilities in your company and your industry are going. The tricky thing is capabilities that seem unimportant today could turn out to be very important in the future because of the differing rates of improvement.

Pisano: Be aware. At the margin, it always seems to make sense to outsource the next highest source of value-added activity. But, over time, those capabilities erode, and you are at the mercy of those few suppliers with capabilities.

CIO.com: Innovation is inextricably tied to IT in many industries today. Will the increasing offshoring of internal technology operations further erode American competitiveness?

Shih: A lot of IT outsourcing has resulted in the development of strong software capabilities in other parts of the world. It has accelerated the diffusion of this capability. The strong software commons in India and, increasingly, China bodes well for products for which software is an important component.

Pisano: Yes, no question about it. But, I don't want CIOs to come away with the message that we are against outsourcing—or that they should never outsource. That's not what we are saying at all. There is a lot of great IT capability in many different corners of the world, and it would be crazy for a CIO not to be thinking about how to take advantage of those. At the same time, they need to think about what they really need to have geographically close. It is clear that for IT professionals, the world is becoming a much more competitive place. If you are in that field, you are going to have to be continually improving your skill sets. And, if you are company in that space, you have to be innovating. You can't compete on cost.

CIO.com: What advice would you offer CIOs and IT decision makers on striking the right balance between insourcing, outsourcing, and offshoring?

Shih: One global head of IT of a large airline company once told me, "You can't outsource your thinking." I think that captures one of the essences of what we're saying. It's important to understand where your capabilities come from, and how you sustain them.

CIO.com: The focus in many companies—in terms of IT investment—continues to be cost savings. Can you give CIOs a financially based argument that they can take to their executive teams and boards against offshoring higher value capabilities?

Pisano: Sometimes there is no case against outsourcing. There are strong skills at very good costs available from lots of places. But, where they have to be careful is when they are outsourcing capabilities that become critical to the future. Can you justify that in some spreadsheet financial analysis? Probably. But standard tools of financial analysis are very limited when it comes to evaluating these kinds of capability-creating decisions. You need management with judgment.

Shih: This is a classic short-term versus long-term investment question. Long-term investments in capability maintenance and development are no different than other long-term investments in productive capacity. The harder thing to evaluate is the investment in the health of the commons. This is a classic "tragedy of the commons" problem; firms don't see the short-term benefits of such investments. That's one of the challenges. Our financial tools don't have a good way of capturing this.

| "*Many organisations are turning to sourcing for achieving short term cost savings or other financial benefits.*"

Outsourcing Increases Corporate Profitability
Capgemini Consulting

Capgemini Consulting is a management consulting, outsourcing, and professional services firm headquartered in Paris, France. In the following viewpoint, the author presents results of a survey showing that lowering business costs is the primary driver for companies that outsource work to third-party vendors. According to the results from a survey of executives from large national and multinational companies, the viewpoint states, businesses also outsource as a way to shift their focus to core activities—which in turn, helps improve product standards. The survey also found, according to the viewpoint, that companies weigh a number of factors and risks—like increased dependency on suppliers—when deciding on an outsourcing strategy.

As you read, consider the following questions:

1. According to the author, what are some of the reasons that financial services organizations cite as important for outsourcing?

"Outsourcing Strategy Survey 2009–2010," Capgemini Consulting survey, October 2009. The information contained in this document is proprietary. Copyright © 2010 Capgemini. All rights reserved. Reproduced by permission.

2. What is only perceived as risk when establishing an SSC, according to Capgemini?
3. According to predictions cited by the author, what are important drivers for more organizations to enter into strategic partnerships?

Cost reduction remains the most important reason for sourcing. In line with other surveys this shows that organisations still associate sourcing with cost effectiveness. As a result of the current economic downturn, organisations feel the pressure to reduce costs and reduce working capital. Many organisations are turning to sourcing for achieving short term cost savings or other financial benefits.

Companies Outsource to Lower Costs

Manufacturers indicate that they use both sourcing strategies to focus more on their core business, which results in cost reduction and improved business focus. Products are tangible and the pressure to set new product standards is high. Some of the manufacturing organisations even mentioned they are driven by customer pressure to improve standards and, therefore, source processes.

Financial services organisations indicate that cost reduction and headcount reduction are important reasons for sourcing. Headcount reduction was mentioned as a reason for an SSC [shared service center] more often in comparison to other industries.

Energy and utilities organisations indicated that the most important reason for establishing an SSC is to improve quality. They find this more important than cost reduction and improved business focus. The energy and utilities industry also sees outsourcing as a gateway to knowledge and competence.

Companies Weigh Risks

Overall, the perceived risks of outsourcing correspond to those of an SSC. We did, however, find four key differences.

- Organisations choose their sourcing strategy based on risk mitigation. The perceived risks of outsourcing are related to the commercial relationship between the insourcer and the outsourcer. Organisations anticipate a possible lock-in with the supplier. The tangible benefits of the outsourcing deal may be outweighed by the costs and perceived risks associated with outsourcing.

- By selecting an SSC, organisations want to ensure proximity to the business, avoiding dependency on external suppliers and loss of knowledge. As a participant mentioned, "Speed and flexibility is crucial to us. In this case, the cost reduction created by outsourcing was insignificant compared to the impact of not delivering to our customer on time".

- Organisations have a strong focus on quality when setting up an SSC. As mentioned before, organisations see an SSC as a vehicle to improve quality. At the same time, they perceive loss of quality as the highest risk. In the preparation of an SSC the key question is: how do organisations ensure the desired quality level?

- Loss of business alignment is only perceived as a risk when establishing an SSC. We did expect to find that loss of business alignment was also perceived as a risk of outsourcing. This was not the case. Whilst, by outsourcing a process, the distance between service provider and customer increases, it seems that organisations do not perceive this distance to be a major issue.

Outsourcing Risks Vary

Manufacturing organisations perceive dependency on the supplier and loss of knowledge as high risks of outsourcing. As mentioned before, manufacturers have a strong drive to reduce costs and improve business focus. Loss of knowledge and dependency on the supplier are perceived as road blocks to achieving these goals.

Financial services organisations perceive the loss of business alignment as a high risk of establishing an SSC, far higher in comparison to the other industries surveyed. Financial services organisations are service providers and see information and employees as valuable assets. Processes within financial services organisations are also highly interwoven, in particular HR [human resources] and IT [information technology] processes. These processes have to be disentangled, which could cause loss of business alignment between the organisation and the SSC.

Energy and utilities organisations mainly bring in external suppliers to obtain knowledge, not to improve quality. In comparing the reasons and risks of sourcing in both the SSC and the outsourcing modes, we found a correlation between the reasons for one sourcing mode and risks of the other. Improving quality, for example, is the most important reason for establishing an SSC but the potential for reduced quality is perceived as the highest risk of outsourcing. Gaining knowledge, for example, is an important reason for agreeing to outsource services but losing knowledge is seen to be a high risk when establishing an SSC.

Cost Reduction Is Most Important

The reasons and risks associated with each sourcing mode have not been changed by current events. Cost reduction remains the most important reason for organisations to (out)source.

The survey results show expected quality from outsourcing is lower than moving to an SSC. This might be perception as outsourcing is often managed through performance contracts unlike SSCs.

Many differences between organisations are caused by their business strategy. Do they have a 'customer intimacy', 'product leadership' or 'operational excellence' strategy? In our opinion, the right reasons for choosing whether to use the outsourcing or SSC mode are those which best align with your business strategy. It helps to consider several sourcing modes, in the analysis and definition phase, when identifying the right sourcing strategy.

Some organisations take multi-sourcing to the extreme, leading to complex onshore and offshore multivendor relations.

Although only a small number of participants mentioned innovation as a reason for outsourcing, we expect this number to increase in the coming years. Due to pressure to differentiate from competitors, organisations are entering into more strategic partnerships, for which knowledge transfer and innovation are important drivers. In our opinion, the full added value of innovation by outsourcing is not yet discovered, but this is just a matter of time.

| "Outsourcing . . . can wreck your
business and cost you a bundle."

Outsourcing Does Not Always Increase Corporate Profitability

Michael Hiltzik

Michael Hiltzik is an author and Pulitzer Prize–winning writer for the Los Angeles Times. *In the following viewpoint, Hiltzik uses the Boeing company and its 787 Dreamliner as an example of how a company's outsourcing strategy can backfire, creating large cost overruns and serious quality-control issues. In an effort to cut costs, Hiltzik relates, Boeing outsourced the manufacture and design of key aircraft components to subcontractors all over the country, and also to companies in Italy, Sweden, China, and South Korea. Not every dollar spent on outsourcing results in cost savings, Hiltzik maintains, and a flawed outsourcing strategy led to Boeing going billions of dollars over budget.*

As you read, consider the following questions:

1. According to the author, what percentage of the 787 Dreamliner was made with foreign parts?

Michael Hiltzik, "787 Dreamliner Teaches Boeing Costly Lesson on Outsourcing," *Los Angeles Times*, February 15, 2011. Copyright © 2011 by Los Angeles Times. All rights reserved. Reproduced by permission.

2. A 2001 analysis by a Boeing senior technical fellow pre-dicted what, according to Hiltzik?

3. According to the author, what did Jim Albaugh, Boeing commercial aviation chief, tell Seattle University business students about what the company had learned from its outsourcing failure with the 787 Dreamliner?

The biggest mistake people make when talking about the outsourcing of U.S. jobs by U.S. companies is to treat it as a moral issue.

Sure, it's immoral to abandon your loyal American workers in search of cheap labor overseas. But the real problem with out-sourcing, if you don't think it through, is that it can wreck your business and cost you a bundle.

Case in point: Boeing Co. and its 787 Dreamliner.

The next-generation airliner is billions of dollars over budget and about three years late; the first paying passengers won't be boarding until this fall [2011], if then. Some of the delay stems from the plane's advances in design, engineering and material, which made it harder to build. A two-month machinists strike in 2008 didn't help.

But much of the blame belongs to the company's quantum leap in farming out the design and manufacture of crucial com-ponents to suppliers around the nation and in foreign countries such as Italy, Sweden, China, and South Korea. Boeing's dream was to save money. The reality is that it would have been cheaper to keep a lot of this work in-house.

Lack of Oversight

The 787 has more foreign-made content—30%—than any other Boeing plane, according to the Society of Professional Engineering Employees in Aerospace, the union representing Boeing engineers. That compares with just over 5% in the com-pany's workhorse 747 airliner.

Excessive Downsizing Raises Costs

There is a *minimum* level of work that *must* be accomplished in-house if a company is to remain in business. In addition, very different designs may be needed for different assembly sequences at multiple sites, whether they be within a large corporation or at someone else's factory. Excessive downsizing can lead to an increase in costs; it can also reduce a company below the critical mass of technology needed to develop future product to stay in business. Work may need to be undertaken *outside* defined core competencies merely to ensure that the staff and facilities are available to perform work that *is* defined to be within core competencies. It can also be far more *profitable* to add work to fully utilize existing facilities than to sell off the facilities and out-source the work. The fate of the former Douglas Aircraft Company, which was reduced to a systems integrator in the early 1970s by excessive outsourcing of DC-10 production, is a clear indicator of what will happen to other companies which fail to sustain the conditions under which it is possible to launch *new* products. It is hoped that this sacrifice can save the new and expanded Boeing from a similar fate.

L.J. Hart-Smith, "Out-Sourced Profits—the Cornerstone of Successful Subcontracting," 2001.

Boeing's goal, it seems, was to convert its storied aircraft factory near Seattle to a mere assembly plant, bolting together modules designed and produced elsewhere as though from kits.

The drawbacks of this approach emerged early. Some of the pieces manufactured by far-flung suppliers didn't fit together. Some subcontractors couldn't meet their output quotas, creating huge production logjams when critical parts weren't available in the necessary sequence.

Rather than follow its old model of providing parts subcontractors with detailed blueprints created at home, Boeing gave suppliers less detailed specifications and required them to create their own blueprints.

Some then farmed out their engineering to their own subcontractors, Mike Bair, the former head of the 787 program, said at a meeting of business leaders in Washington state in 2007. That further reduced Boeing's ability to supervise design and manufacture. At least one major supplier didn't even have an engineering department when it won its contract, according to an analysis of the 787 by the European consortium Airbus, Boeing's top global competitor.

Boeing executives now admit that the company's aggressive outsourcing put it in partnership with suppliers that weren't up to the job. They say Boeing didn't recognize that sending so much work abroad would demand more intensive management from the home plant, not less.

"We gave work to people that had never really done this kind of technology before, and then we didn't provide the oversight that was necessary," Jim Albaugh, the company's commercial aviation chief, told business students at Seattle University. "In hindsight, we spent a lot more money in trying to recover than we ever would have spent if we tried to keep many of the key technologies closer to Boeing. The pendulum swung too far."

Extreme Appetite for Outsourcing

Some critics trace Boeing's extreme appetite for outsourcing to the regimes of Harry Stonecipher and Alan Mulally.

Stonecipher became Boeing's president and later chief executive after its 1997 merger with McDonnell-Douglas, where he had been CEO. Mulally took over the commercial aviation group the following year and is now CEO of Ford. The merged company appeared to prize short-term profits over the development of its engineering expertise, and began to view outsourcing too myopically as a cost-saving process.

That's not to say that outsourcing never makes sense—it's a good way to make use of the precision skills of specialty manufacturers, which would be costly to duplicate. But Boeing's experience shows that it's folly to think that every dollar spent on outsourcing means a cost savings on the finished product.

Boeing can't say it wasn't warned. As early as 2001, L.J. Hart-Smith, a Boeing senior technical fellow, produced a prescient analysis projecting that excessive outsourcing would raise Boeing's costs and steer profits to its subcontractors.

Among the least profitable jobs in aircraft manufacturing, he pointed out, is final assembly—the job Boeing proposed to retain. But its subcontractors would benefit from free technical assistance from Boeing if they ran into problems, and would hang on to the highly profitable business of producing spare parts over the decades-long life of the aircraft. Their work would be almost risk-free, Hart-Smith observed, because if they ran into really insuperable problems they would simply be bought out by Boeing.

What do you know? In 2009, Boeing spent about $1 billion in cash and credit to take over the underperforming fuselage manufacturing plant of Vought Aircraft Industries, which had contributed to the years of delays.

Costly Outsourcing Lessons

"I didn't dream all this up," Hart-Smith, who is retired, told me from his home in his native Australia. "I'd lived it at Douglas Aircraft."

As an engineer at McDonnell-Douglas' Long Beach plant, he said, he saw how extensive outsourcing of the DC-10 airliner allowed the suppliers to make all the profits but impoverished the prime manufacturer.

"I warned Boeing not to make the same mistake. Everybody there seemed to get the message, except top management."

The company's unions have also kept singing an anti-outsourcing chorale. "We've been raising these questions for five years," says Tom McCarty, the president of the Boeing engineers' union. "How do you control the project, and how do you justify giving these major pieces of work to relatively inexperienced suppliers? There's no track record of being able to do this."

It would be easier to dismiss these concerns as those of unions trying to hold on to their jobs if they hadn't been validated by the words of Boeing executives themselves. A company spokeswoman told me that it's not giving up on outsourcing—"we're a global company," she says—but is hoping for a "continued refinement of that business model." Yet Albaugh and other executives acknowledge that they've blundered.

"We didn't want to make the investment that needed to be made, and we asked our partners to make that investment," Albaugh told his Seattle University audience. The company now recognizes that "we need to know how to do every major system on the airplane better than our suppliers do."

One would have thought that the management of the world's leading aircraft manufacturer would know that going in, before handing over millions of dollars of work to companies that couldn't turn out a Tab A that fit reliably into Slot A. On-the-job training for senior executives, it seems, can be *very* expensive.

Periodical and Internet Sources Bibliography

The following articles have been chosen to supplement the diverse views presented in this chapter.

Tony Bradley	"Is IT Outsourcing Worth It?," *PCWorld*, June 19, 2012.
Thursday Bram	"Times When Outsourcing Is a Good Fit for Your Company," *Investopedia*, June 4, 2012. www .investopedia.com.
Jeff Haden	"The 7 Biggest Outsourcing Mistakes to Avoid," CBS News, May 16, 2011. www.cbsnews.com.
Ben W. Heineman	"In Defense of Responsible Offshoring and Outsourcing," *Harvard Business Review*, February 22, 2012.
Geoffrey James	"Top 10 Reasons Offshoring Is Bad for Business," CBS News, June 27, 2011. www.cbsnews.com.
Knowledge@Wharton	"Research Roundup: The 'Flip Side' of Open Innovation, Productivity Losses from Bad Weather and Assessing the Risks of Outsourcing," February 1, 2012. http://knowledge .wharton.upenn.edu.
Las Vegas Review-Journal	"Public-Sector Outsourcing," April 14, 2011.
M.H.	"Outsourcing Is So Last Year," *Economist*, May 11, 2012.
Panos Mourdoukoutas	"The Unintended Consequences of Outsourcing," *Forbes*, December 9, 2011.
Kristin Samuelson	"Outsourcing, Offshoring: The Good, Bad and Ugly," *Chicago Tribune*, January 29, 2012.
Alix Stuart	"Offshore Outsourcing: For Smaller Companies, Too," *CFO*, May 25, 2011.

OPPOSING
VIEWPOINTS®
SERIES

CHAPTER 3

What Impact Has Outsourcing Had on the US Economy?

Chapter Preface

One out of every three manufacturing jobs—roughly six million—disappeared from the American manufacturing landscape in the decade ending in 2009, according to the Bureau of Labor Statistics. And despite modest gains in some years, overall employment in manufacturing has been on the decline since the 1980s. In fact, the decline as a share of total manufacturing jobs in the 2000s has surpassed the rate of job loss during the Great Depression of the 1930s.

While some economists have attributed the loss of manufacturing jobs to greater efficiency and productivity, a March 2012 report published by a nonpartisan think tank called the Information Technology & Innovation Foundation offers a different explanation. In the report, titled "Worse than the Great Depression: What Experts Are Missing About American Manufacturing Decline," the authors assert that the decline in American manufacturing jobs is due to the fact that manufacturing as a sector lost output as the result of its declining ability to effectively compete in the global marketplace. The authors of the report point out that foreign mercantilist policies as well as lower corporate tax rates and incentives in other countries have harmed the US manufacturing sector's ability to compete with global counterparts. According to the report, there were more unemployed Americans (12.8 million) in January 2012 than there were Americans working in the manufacturing sector. The report also maintains that government statistics have overstated US manufacturing productivity, and that the methods used to calculate that productivity have been flawed.

Many economists and commentators also argue that offshore outsourcing has had a significant impact on the overall decline of manufacturing jobs in the United States. According to Howard Wial, a nonresident senior fellow at the Brookings Institution's Metropolitan Policy Program, another reason for the loss of US manufacturing jobs is the various incentives that have made off-shoring work to low-wage countries more attractive to US companies. In the February 2012 article, "Manufacturing Job Loss Is Not Inevitable," Wial points out that "manipulated currencies" and "artificially low wages of China and some other low-wage countries" lured manufacturers interested in reducing labor costs. In the article, Wial states that with the right kind of policies, US policy makers could have made offshoring less attractive to manufacturers by "taking a harder line against China's currency manipulation and wage suppression."

Regardless of the driving factors behind offshoring, many believe that outsourcing has not only gutted America's manufacturing sector, some also argue that it is damaging other economic sectors as well. Forrester Research estimates that by 2015, 3.5 million US white-collar jobs—in fields like engineering, computer programming, and research and development—will have moved offshore to lower-wage countries like India, China, and Mexico. Many believe that this exodus of white-collar jobs has already begun and that it is having a damaging effect on American workers and the nation's ability to compete in an increasingly high-tech global marketplace.

Others say that outsourcing has not had a negative impact on the US economy, but that it has actually helped strengthen some industries. Some point to the information technology (IT) sector as an example—since IT work often can be performed off site, IT workers are able to telecommute with ease and to market themselves on a global scale. Some also say that the increase in outsourcing has created more job opportunities as companies seem more open to hiring outside help for IT and other types of work.

In the viewpoints that follow, writers debate the wide-ranging impact that offshore outsourcing has had on American workers, the US economy, the nation's overall competitiveness, and the long-term outlook for American companies that are trying to compete globally. While the writers differ in their views, most seem to agree that outsourcing has impacted the US economy to a greater or lesser degree, and that it will continue to impact individual workers, US companies, and the nation's economy in the years to come.

| "Outsourcing . . . is a lose-lose situation for American employees, American businesses, and the American government."

Offshore Outsourcing Has Damaged the US Economy

Paul Craig Roberts

Paul Craig Roberts is an author, syndicated columnist, and former assistant secretary of the US Treasury. In the following viewpoint he argues that short-sighted outsourcing strategies and policies are contributing to unprecedented US unemployment, economic decline, and the erosion of America as a superpower. Roberts also points out that outsourcing has resulted in record unemployment in the engineering field and lower enrollments in technical and scientific studies at American universities as corporations continue to replace US employees with foreign workers through guest worker visa programs. The result, Roberts says, is that American corporations are handing over their technological advantage to foreign companies while reducing their own businesses to a brand name with a sales force.

As you read, consider the following questions:
1. According to a University of California study cited by Roberts, how many white-collar jobs are vulnerable to offshore outsourcing?
2. On the basis of US Department of Labor research cited by the author, what often happens to displaced workers if they are lucky enough to find work again?
3. What do Ron and Anil Hira say, as cited by Roberts, about US corporations' use of offshore operations to gain a foothold in Asian markets?

Is offshore outsourcing good or harmful for America? To convince Americans of outsourcing's benefits, corporate outsourcers sponsor misleading one-sided "studies."

Only a small handful of people have looked objectively at the issue. These few and the large number of Americans whose careers have been destroyed by outsourcing have a different view of outsourcing's impact. But so far there has been no debate, just a shouting down of skeptics as "protectionists."

Now comes an important new book, *Outsourcing America*, published by the American Management Association. The authors, two brothers, Ron and Anil Hira, are experts on the subject. One is a professor at the Rochester Institute of Technology, and the other is a professor at Simon Fraser University.

The authors note that despite the enormity of the stakes for all Americans, a state of denial exists among policy makers and outsourcing's corporate champions about the adverse effects on the US. The Hira brothers succeed in their task of interjecting harsh reality where delusion has ruled.

In what might be an underestimate, a University of California study concludes that 14 million white-collar jobs are vulnerable to being outsourced offshore. These are not only call-center operators, customer service and back-office jobs, but also information technology, accounting, architecture, advanced engineering design, news reporting, stock analysis, and medical and legal services. The authors note that these are the jobs of the American Dream, the jobs of upward mobility that generate the bulk of the tax revenues that fund our education, health, infrastructure, and social security systems.

The loss of these jobs "is fool's gold for companies." Corporate America's short-term mentality, stemming from bonuses tied to quarterly results, is causing US companies to lose not only their best employees—their human capital—but also the consumers who buy their products. Employees displaced by foreigners and left unemployed or in lower-paid work have a reduced presence in the consumer market. They provide fewer retirement savings for new investment.

Bad News for US Jobs

No-think economists assume that new, better jobs are on the way for displaced American's, but no economists can identify these jobs. The authors point out that "the track record for the re-employment of displaced US workers is abysmal: "The Department of Labor reports that more than one in three workers who are displaced remains unemployed, and many of those who are lucky enough to find jobs take major pay cuts. Many former manufacturing workers who were displaced a decade ago because of manufacturing that went offshore took training courses and found jobs in the information technology sector. They are now facing the unenviable situation of having their second career disappear overseas."

American economists are so inattentive to outsourcing's perils that they fail to realize that the same incentive that leads to the outsourcing of one tradable good or service holds for all tradable goods and services. In the 21st century the US economy has only been able to create jobs in nontradable domestic services—the hallmark of a third-world labor force.

Prior to the advent of offshore outsourcing, US employees were shielded against low wage foreign labor. Americans worked

Outsourcing White-Collar Jobs

Offshore outsourcing, which is one form of globalization, has adversely affected particular white-collar jobs: information technology (IT) occupations (e.g., computer programmers, systems analysts, and software engineers) and IT-enabled occupations (e.g., telemarketers and accounting clerks). Factory workers continue to experience job anxiety as their ranks further dwindle at the same time that the U.S. population overall reaps benefits from international trade (e.g., lower priced goods for consumers).

Some observers believe that the United States has seen just the tip of the offshoring iceberg. By one estimate, 22% to 29% of all U.S. jobs possess characteristics that will make them susceptible to outsourcing to globally dispersed talent within a 10- to 20-year time frame. Others expect that firms will lose enthusiasm for offshore outsourcing due to various reasons (e.g., less-than-anticipated cost savings, and customer dissatisfaction) and consequently will use the business practice more strategically.

Linda Levine, Congressional Research Service, August 6, 2007.

with more capital and better technology, and their higher productivity protected their higher wages.

Outsourcing forces Americans to "compete head-to-head with foreign workers" by "undermining US workers' primary competitive advantage over foreign workers: their physical presence in the US" and "by providing those overseas workers with the same technologies."

The result is a lose-lose situation for American employees, American businesses, and the American government.

Outsourcing has brought about record unemployment in engineering fields and a major drop in university enrollments in technical and scientific disciplines. Even many of the remaining jobs are being filled by lower paid foreigners brought in on H-1b and L-1 visas. American employees are discharged after being forced to train their foreign replacements.

Eroding US Competitiveness

US corporations justify their offshore operations as essential to gaining a foothold in emerging Asian markets. The Hira brothers believe this is self-delusion. "There is no evidence that they will be able to outcompete local Chinese and Indian companies, who are very rapidly assimilating the technology and know-how from the local US plants. In fact, studies show that Indian IT companies have been consistently outcompeting their US counterparts, even in US markets. Thus, it is time for CEOs to start thinking about whether they are fine with their own jobs being outsourced as well."

The authors note that the national security implications of outsourcing "have been largely ignored."

Outsourcing is rapidly eroding America's superpower status. Beginning in 2002 the US began running trade deficits in advanced technology products with Asia, Mexico and Ireland. As these countries are not leaders in advanced technology, the deficits obviously stem from US offshore manufacturing. In effect, the US is giving away its technology, which is rapidly being captured, while US firms reduce themselves to a brand name with a sales force.

In an appendix, the authors provide a devastating exposé of the three "studies" that have been used to silence doubts about offshore outsourcing—the Global Insight study (March 2004) for the Information Technology Association of America [ITAA], the Catherine Mann study (December 2003) for the Institute for International Economics, and the McKinsey Global Institute study (August 2003).

The ITAA is a lobbying group for outsourcing. The ITAA spun the results of the study by releasing only the executive summary to reporters who agreed not to seek outside opinion prior to writing their stories.

Mann's study is "an unreasonably optimistic forecast based on faulty logic and a poor understanding of technology and strategy."

The McKinsey report "should be viewed as a self-interested lobbying document that presents an unrealistically optimistic estimate of the impact of offshore outsourcing and an undeveloped and politically unviable solution to the problems they identify."

Outsourcing America is a powerful work. Only fools will continue clinging to the premise that outsourcing is good for America.

| "The U.S. is the 3rd largest exporter and the number one manufacturing economy in the world."

Offshore Outsourcing Has Not Damaged the US Economy

Michael Newkirk

Michael Newkirk is the director of global manufacturing and sup-ply chain product marketing for SAS Institute Inc., a software pro-vider based in Cary, North Carolina. In the following viewpoint, Newkirk asserts that the United States is still the global leader in manufacturing despite some reports that suggest that China and India are outpacing American manufacturing. Newkirk also pres-ents statistics to debunk the myth that multinational corporations are destroying American jobs by investing overseas. Newkirk high-lights the fact that many multinational companies, such as General Electric, continue to invest in their US operations to fulfill demand overseas. This continued investment, according to Newkirk, has re-sulted in the preservation of skilled, high-paying US jobs.

As you read, consider the following questions:

1. How does the United States rank as an exporter in the global economy, according to data cited by Newkirk?

Michael Newkirk, "Is Manufacturing Dead in America?," *IndustryWeek*, January 26, 2012.

2. According to statistics cited by the author, how many Americans did multinational corporations employ domestically in 2008, and what percentage of these workers were employed in direct manufacturing?
3. From a workforce standpoint, why do companies invest overseas, according to Newkirk?

I was privileged to attend the National Association of Manufacturers (NAM) Board of Directors meeting in Washington, D.C. recently. Attended by some 300 senior executives of American manufacturing companies, it was like a who's-who in brand names anyone would recognize.

Many economists have stated that you cannot achieve and sustain economic leadership without a robust manufacturing sector. And yes, the conventional wisdom of the day is all about the decline of U.S. manufacturing. In 2012, we will increasingly hear the claim that companies are "shipping jobs overseas" with the implication that we need more laws and regulations from the candidates that promote this idea.

But what I heard at the NAM Board meeting were facts about U.S. manufacturing that tell a much different story:

U.S. Manufacturing Leads the World

The U.S. is still the leading manufacturing nation on earth, while China and India are growing much faster in their manufacturing. This is good, not bad. They need to grow. They each have huge populations and an emerging middle-class demographic that demands a better standard of living. The economic pie of world wealth is not fixed, it is dynamic and getting bigger. We should be glad they are growing their middle class. But this hardly means the U.S. is becoming irrelevant in manufacturing. The U.S. produced 19% of the worldwide value-added manufacturing output in 2008 and about 22% of that was exported. The U.S. is the 3rd largest exporter and the number one manufacturing economy in the world.

Multinationals Still Call the United States Home

The U.S. is still the largest economy in the world. The U.S. is still the largest manufacturing economy in the world. It has critical mass, and scalability. The U.S. still has a first-class university system, turning out high-skilled workers. AND it still has a flexible, mobile, productive workforce, with a still decent immigration system. . . .

Multinational corporations like Dow [Chemical Company] still see the U.S. as our hub. Growing overseas is not a threat. The way we structure our global operations reflects that as our overseas operations grow, so does our home base, our hub. Even when we manufacture in other countries, those operations are but satellite spokes from our central hub in the U.S.

Andrew Liveris, Dow Chemical Company,
February 23, 2011.

The percent of GDP [gross domestic product] that manufacturing occupies has remained about the same for the past 30 years. In 1900, 38% of the labor force was involved in farming. By 1990, that fell to 2.6%. Why is that important? Because, over time, farming became much more productive and mechanized and required less labor. Manufacturing labor is similar to farm labor in terms of a slow decline in its share of employment and national output. But adjusting for price changes, the share of GDP for the manufacturing sector has tracked with the overall economy over the past 60 years.

Businesses provide the bulk of taxes that fuel state and local governments. Manufacturers run a close second to services at 20% of business taxation and without a healthy manufacturing base, we would be in a much more precarious position than we are now. In 2008, business taxes accounted for 44% of [the revenues of] state and local governments, other non-business taxes made up 35% and individual income taxes made up just 21%. Raising income taxes on any group of Americans, wealthy or otherwise, will not get us tax revenue like revving the engines of business will produce.

Facts About Overseas Manufacturing

Another myth exploded is the idea that U.S. manufacturing investment abroad destroys U.S. jobs. Consider these facts:

- U.S. multinational corporations (MNCs) employed 22.4 million Americans domestically in 2008 and nearly 12 million were employed directly in manufacturing. Of that 12 million, 7 million worked for MNCs.

- MNC affiliates employed 5.4 million manufacturing workers overseas with nearly half of them employed in high wage countries in Europe or in Canada. Only 10% were in China, less than Germany and France combined.

- From 2000–2008, manufacturing jobs overseas in MNC affiliates increased by only 314,000; this is barely 6% growth and one-third of this was in Europe.

- MNCs with operations in many countries had much higher labor productivity than those with operations in only a few countries ($154K versus $100K average value added).

- Companies invest abroad to serve local markets. U.S. affiliates sold $2.7 trillion in manufactured goods in foreign markets in 2008 and 90% of sales were to local markets not exported back to the U.S.

- Companies invest abroad to seek a skilled workforce, not cheap labor. U.S. manufacturing foreign direct investment (FDI) stood at $541 billion in 2009; 72% by value was in developed countries and U.S. manufacturing investment in

China was only 4 percent of total FDI; 75% of value added of all affiliates was in high-wage countries.

U.S. Companies Still Invest Here

MNCs remain committed to producing in the United States and are investing in the future. Jeff Immelt, Chairman and CEO of GE [General Electric], spoke at the meeting and made a clear, direct statement to this issue. He listed a number of areas where GE has made heavy investments, including expanded locomotive and aircraft engine operations because they have received so many orders overseas. These are skilled, high-paying jobs with long-term prospects as the contracts to produce these complex, highly engineered products run many years.

- Overall, U.S. manufacturing shipments totaled $5.5 trillion in 2008, up 30% from 2000 and MNC sales accounted for about 75% of the total for manufacturing.
- MNC research and development expenditures in the U.S. in 2008 were $236 billion, and 77% or $183 billion was in manufacturing.
- MNCs overseas investments are NOT the cause of the trade deficit. Consider that MNCs exported $507 billion in manufactured goods from the US in 2008. Their affiliates took nearly half of those exports.

Manufactured goods trade accounted for only $72 billion of the $698 billion trade deficit in 2008 and if you exclude petroleum and coal products, MNCs actually produced a trade surplus of $106 billion in 2008.

That was a fire hose of numbers and facts, but we must make the critical decisions about our future based on facts. From my vantage point, that is what leading edge companies are doing, and we must hold our politicians to that standard as well. Day after day, I see U.S. manufacturers like the 100+ year old American manufacturing icon Dow Chemical investing in people and technology to drive out costs, improve quality and gain new customers.

Manufacturing in the U.S. is the engine that has largely pulled not only the U.S. economy out of the ditch, but the world economy as well. And if we don't pay attention to what manufacturers are saying about what hinders them from creating new jobs and innovating new products, we do so at our own peril. Manufacturing is not even in the hospital, let alone dead. But if public officials play fast and loose with the truth and use MNCs, and manufacturing MNCs in particular, as a punching bag, they can certainly make her very sick.

| "Jobs likely to be offshored are relatively low-wage, low-skill jobs while the jobs to be gained through services exporting (and 'inshoring') are relatively high-wage, high-skill jobs."

Offshore Outsourcing Can Favor Some High-Skill Service Providers

J. Bradford Jensen and Lori G. Kletzer

J. Bradford Jensen is a senior fellow at the Peterson Institute for International Economics and an economics and international business professor at Georgetown University. Lori G. Kletzer, a nonresident senior fellow with the Peterson Institute, is vice president for academic affairs and dean of faculty at Colby College in Waterville, Maine. In the following viewpoint, Jensen and Kletzer present findings suggesting that US workers who specialize in high-skill services may benefit from offshore outsourcing. According to the authors, gains in high-wage, high-skill service exporting will help offset the loss of low-wage, low-skill jobs that typically are offshored to low-wage countries. Jensen and Kletzer also predict an increase in high-wage, high-skill production in the manufacturing and tradable services sectors as trade barriers are lowered.

J. Bradford Jensen and Lori G. Kletzer, "Fear and Offshoring: The Scope and Potential Impact of Imports and Exports of Services," Peterson Institute for International Economics, January 2008. Copyright © 2008 by Peterson Institute for International Economics. All rights reserved. Reproduced by permission.

As you read, consider the following questions:

1. According to statistics cited by the authors, how many jobs are at risk of being outsourced to low-wage, labor-abundant countries, and what percentage of these are in manufacturing?
2. On the basis of data presented by the authors, what is the typical annual salary of a worker in a tradable service industry compared with the salary of a worker in a nontradable service industry?
3. According to Jensen and Kletzer, what types of activity are most likely to move offshore?

A number of commentators have provided forecasts of the potential impact of services offshoring. Perhaps the most notable forecast comes from Alan Blinder in an interview that appeared on the front page of the *Wall Street Journal*. Blinder suggests that as many as 40 million jobs could be at risk of being offshored over the next two decades [January 2008–]. He advances the view that American workers should specialize in activities that are "personal" services (i.e., activities delivered face-to-face), because the United States is likely to lose many of the jobs that are "impersonal" (i.e., activities delivered at a distance).

While we agree with Blinder and other commentators that the number of activities that can be provided at a distance, and are thus tradable, is large, we will argue that these other commentators miss two important pieces of the story:

1. Comparative advantage suggests about one-third of tradable service activities are at risk of being offshored to low-wage, labor-abundant countries like India and China.
2. The United States is currently a net exporter of services and likely to gain relatively high-wage, high-skill jobs through increased exports of services.

By omitting these considerations, the discussion becomes unduly alarmist, with the policy advice (e.g., specialize in "personal" services) potentially misguided. . . .

The number of jobs at risk of being offshored to low-wage, labor-abundant countries is about 15–20 million with many of these jobs (about 40 percent) in the manufacturing sector (long considered "at risk"). . . . Job "losses" will be offset by job "gains" from services exporting. Further . . . the jobs likely to be offshored are relatively low-wage, low-skill jobs while the jobs to be gained through services exporting (and "inshoring") are relatively high-wage, high-skill jobs.

Good Prospects Exist

Combined, the evidence we present suggests healthy prospects for American workers specializing in *high-skill* service activities, not nontradable "personal" services, because of their export potential and attractive wage premiums.

The basis for our conclusion is a threshold (evident in the data) for activities that are being lost to low-wage, labor-abundant countries in manufacturing and a similar threshold for activities where US exports increase in both manufacturing and services.

This threshold is evidence that comparative advantage is indeed functioning—the United States imports low-wage, low-skill goods and services and exports high-wage, high-skill goods and services. Further, most employment in tradable service activities is above this threshold and thus most workers in tradable service activities are unlikely to face significant competition from low-wage, labor-abundant countries any time soon. Indeed, many of the firms and workers in tradable services are likely to benefit from increased services trade by exporting. This notion is critical to understand the impact of services offshoring on the US labor market and is explained in more detail below.

This policy brief reports evidence from an ongoing project at the Peterson Institute, other recent studies examining the service sector, and recent research examining the impact of globalization on the manufacturing sector to present a more comprehensive picture of the likely impact of services offshoring on US workers and firms. It reports on a novel characterization of "tradability" that can be applied to occupations, as well as to services and manufacturing industries.

Increased Export of Services Benefits

This policy brief draws the following conclusions:

- Many service activities—movie and music recording production, securities and commodities trading, software, and engineering services as examples—appear to be traded within the United States and thus are at least potentially tradable internationally. Approximately 14 percent of the workforce is in service industries classified as tradable. By comparison, about 12 percent of the workforce is in manufacturing industries classified as tradable. When workers in tradable occupations (such as computer programmers in the retail banking industry or medical transcriptionists in the healthcare industry) in nontradable industries are included, the share of the workforce in tradable service activities is even higher.

- While many service activities appear tradable, we anticipate that only about one-third of the jobs in these activities will face meaningful competition from low-wage countries (or risk being offshored) in the medium term.

- Tradable service jobs, such as those at engineering or research and development (R&D) firms, are good jobs. Workers in tradable service activities have higher than average earnings. Part of this premium is due to workers in these activities having higher educational attainment than other workers, but even controlling for differences in education and other personal characteristics, workers in tradable service activities have 10 percent higher earnings. Within the set of professional service industries, a worker in a tradable industry and a tradable occupation has earnings almost 20 percent higher than a similar professional service worker in a nontradable industry and occupation.

- High earnings in tradable service activities do not mean that these jobs will be "lost" to low-wage countries. High-wage, high-skill activities are consistent with US comparative advantage. In the manufacturing sector, it is low-wage, labor-intensive industries like apparel that are most vulnerable to low-wage import competition. The United States continues to have strong export performance in high-wage, skill-intensive manufacturing industries.

- The United States currently exports high-wage, high-skill services like computer software and satellite telecommunications services. Most commentators on the offshoring issue focus on the jobs that will be "lost" to offshoring but neglect that the United States has comparative advantage in many service activities. Increased exports of services (and "inshoring") are likely to benefit many US firms and workers.

- As many as two-thirds of tradable business service jobs are skilled enough to be consistent with US comparative advantage. US service workers and firms are likely to be beneficiaries of increased trade in services through increased export opportunities.

- To date, there is little evidence of trade in services influencing labor market outcomes. Net employment growth in the average tradable service activities is roughly the same as net employment growth in nontradable service activities. Median wage growth in tradable service occupations is nearly equal to wage growth in the average nontradable occupation. Rates of job displacement in tradable service activities are no greater than nontradable service activities.

- Many impediments exist to trade in services, ranging from language and cultural differences to regulation to technological barriers. These impediments are likely to protect US firms and workers from import competition but are also likely to impede US firms and workers from exporting. These impediments reduce the gains to the United States (and the rest of the world) from trade in services and the increased living standards that result. While potentially more difficult than reducing tariff barriers, harmonizing regulations and expanding mutual recognition of professional standards and accreditation are important policy objectives to increase the benefits of trade in services. . . .

A Large Share of Total Employment

A significant share of total employment is in tradable service industries. For example, more workers are in tradable industries in the services sector than in manufacturing. The share of total employment in tradable professional services alone is 13.7 percent, while the share of employment in tradable manufacturing industries is 12.4 percent. Some big services sectors—education, healthcare, personal services, and public administration—do in fact have low shares of employment in tradable industries. However, because the services sector is much larger than the manufacturing sector, the number of workers potentially exposed to international trade in services is actually larger than the number of exposed workers in manufacturing.

Moreover, we will see below that many tradable service activities are consistent with US comparative advantage and a source of high-paying jobs when foreign countries import from (or outsource to) US consulting, finance, marketing, and research activities.

Some worker inputs into service production might be tradable even though the service industry itself is not (computer programming or other back office operations for the retail banking industry). In the aggregate, the share of these sorts of workers— who hold tradable occupations in nontradable industries—is not large, at about 10 percent. However, for business and professional occupations, the share of workers in tradable occupations within nontradable industries is much larger. The typical professional occupation has about 25 percent of its employment in tradable occupations within nontradable industries. To the extent that firms can disentangle intermediate service inputs from the rest of their business, workers in these tradable occupations are exposed to trade, even though their industry is not tradable. . . .

Tradable vs. Nontradable Workers

Workers in tradable sectors have higher education levels and significantly higher wages compared with workers in nontradable sectors and manufacturing. Across all service industries, workers in tradable service industries have annual earnings of approximately $47,000; workers in nontradable service industries have average annual earnings of approximately $30,000. Part of the earnings differential is due to higher education. Workers in tradable service industries are twice as likely to have a college degree and twice as likely to have an advanced degree as workers in manufacturing.

But the higher incomes are not solely a result of higher skill levels—even controlling for differences in skills, workers in tradable service activities, like engineering, R&D labs, software publishing, and management consulting, earn incomes almost 20 percent higher than similar workers in nontradable activities in the same sector. . . .

A Comparative Advantage

Indeed, US service establishments that export tend to be in high-wage industries and within those industries pay higher wages on average, again consistent with the notion that the United States has comparative advantage in tradable services production.

Because the United States has comparative advantage in high-skill, high-wage production, the United States is likely to

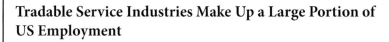

Tradable Service Industries Make Up a Large Portion of US Employment

Tradable industries' share of employment (percent)

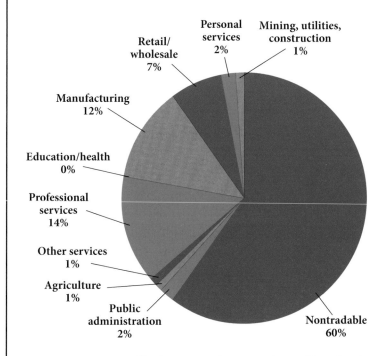

TAKEN FROM: J. Bradford Jensen and Lori G. Kletzer, "'Fear' and Offshoring: The Scope and Potential Impact of Imports and Exports of Services," Peterson Institute for International Economics Policy Brief, January 2008.

retain and indeed increase these activities in both the manufacturing and tradable services sectors as trade barriers diminish.

The evidence suggests that the dividing line between activities where low-wage, labor-abundant countries have comparative advantage and high-wage, high-skill countries have comparative advantage is at industries that have average wages in the United States of about $40,000. While this threshold is not a precise estimate, all of the evidence suggests that this threshold is a useful way to think about the implications of trade in services.

So, while we agree with many commentators that a significant share of employment in the United States is in activities that can be provided at a distance—and are thus tradable—we differ from other commentators in our estimate of how many of the tradable jobs are likely to move offshore. We estimate the number of jobs at risk to offshoring to low-wage, labor-abundant countries is about 15–20 million with many (40–50 percent) of these jobs in the manufacturing sector (long considered "at risk"). We expect low-wage, low-skill job "losses" to be offset by high-wage, high-skill job "gains" from services exporting. A fear of rapid revolutionary change resulting from services offshoring and encouraging US workers to train for nontradable, "personal" service activities seems inappropriate.

Potential notwithstanding, the evidence to date suggests there has been little net employment or median earnings impact of offshoring on US service industries and occupations. For services, there is no discernibly higher risk of job loss in tradable service activities than in nontradable service activities. Given the share of employment in relatively low-wage industries in manufacturing (60 percent) and business services (33 percent), we can anticipate that the risk of manufacturing job loss will remain higher than the risk of service sector job loss.

It seems reasonable to expect that the process of globalization in services will proceed much as it has in manufacturing; relatively low-wage, labor-intensive activities will be the most likely to move offshore. This increased competitive pressure will cause dislocation to workers and firms. But higher-wage, skill-, capital-, and technology-intensive activities will grow through exports to foreign markets. Through both dislocation of import competing industries and exports, the globalization of services production is likely to have productivity-enhancing (and standard of living-increasing) effects similar to the impact of globalization in the manufacturing sector.

Our analysis here acknowledges that services offshoring has potential to cause dislocation in the labor market (as it did in manufacturing), and we do not minimize the individual costs of job dislocation. Our intention is to provide a fuller picture of services trade that underscores how exports of services have the potential to expand high-quality services employment. Trade in services has the potential to contribute significantly to productivity growth within the service sector in the United States (as increased trade contributed to productivity growth in the manufacturing sector). In addition to raising productivity in the United States, trade in services has probably even more potential to improve productivity in developing countries' services sector, where service sector productivity is not as high as in developed countries. Increased trade in services offers significant potential to improve living standards in the United States and around the world.

> "Tech CEOs aren't looking for
> domestic workers. On the contrary,
> they are looking for foreign workers
> who will simply accept lower wages
> and fewer workplace rights than
> Americans."

Offshore Outsourcing Negatively Impacts High-Skill Service Providers

David Sirota

David Sirota is an author, nationally syndicated columnist, and radio host. In the following viewpoint, Sirota takes issue with the argument that corporations are forced to hire foreign workers due to a shortage of American engineers and high-tech workers. The reality, he says, is that corporations misuse the H-1B guest worker visa program to replace American workers by importing lower-wage foreign workers. Sirota also asserts that corporations are not using the H-1B visa program as a way to attract high-skilled foreign workers but rather as a way to offshore America's entire high-tech industry. Sirota also is highly critical of US president Barack Obama's support of the guest worker visa program.

David Sirota, "Obama's High-Tech Labor Lies," *Salon*, February 6, 2012. This article first appeared in Salon.com, at http://www.salon.com. An online version remains in the Salon archives. Reprinted with permission.

As you read, consider the following questions:

1. According to Sirota why is there currently "a generation of jobless engineers"?
2. What does the author say is the median salary for an H-1B holder and how does it compare with that of a skilled domestic worker?
3. Who made up the majority of the top ten H-1B holders in 2011, according to Sirota?

A few days after the *New York Times'* (embarrassingly belated and deeply flawed) article on Apple's Chinese production facilities reignited a national discussion about offshore outsourcing, President Obama was confronted during a Google+ "hang out" about why during a brutal unemployment crisis his administration continues to support expanding the H-1B visa program that allows tech companies to annually import thousands of low-wage engineers from abroad. In his stunning answer, the president first expresses bewilderment that any American high-tech engineer could be out of work, because he says that "what industry tells me is that they don't have enough (domestic) highly skilled engineers" and that "the word that we're getting is that somebody (a domestic engineer) in a high-tech field should be able to find something right away." He then goes on to insist that the H-1B program is "reserved only for those companies who say they cannot find somebody in (a) particular field" and that it shouldn't apply to industries where "there are a lot of highly skilled American workers" looking for a job because he says his administration is focused on "encourag(ing) more American engineers to be placed" in open positions.

For a single news cycle, the interchange made headlines focused on the president's subsequent request that the questioner send her husband's resume to the White House. But as heartwarming as that human interest angle was, it buried the real news in the interchange: namely, that Obama showed himself to be either wholly ignorant of the reality facing high-tech workers today, or simply willing to echo the self-serving lies of his high-tech CEO friends. Whichever it is, the president's claims are clearly at odds with the basic facts of the high-tech labor market.

Though the unemployment rate for the high-tech industry is certainly lower than the overall unemployment rate, the sector is far from the full-employment status that tech CEOs claim. No matter what the industry is "telling" Obama, there remain thousands of highly skilled engineers in America who are either underemployed thanks to tech companies use of the controversial "permatemp" status, or completely out of work. That's because ... despite the political rhetoric to the contrary, our universities are producing far more Science, Technology, Engineering and Math (STEM) workers than allegedly worker-starved tech companies are *willing* to employ. Indeed, a generation of jobless engineers exists not because, as tech CEOs insist, they don't possess the skills to fill open jobs, but because those tech CEOs aren't looking for domestic workers. On the contrary, they are looking for foreign workers who will simply accept lower wages and fewer workplace rights than Americans.

Cheaper Foreign Workers

That brings us to the president's comments about the H-1B program—an instrument so antithetical to the interests of American workers that India's Commerce Minister officially christened it the "outsourcing visa" in 2007. As Rochester Institute of Technology professor Ron Hira has expertly documented in congressional testimony and detailed reports, this visa both allows American high-tech companies to replace their domestic workers with cheaper foreign workers, and also allows foreign outsourcing firms to move huge swaths of America's existing high-tech industry offshore for the long haul.

In the first scenario, which I reported extensively on in my 2008 book *The Uprising*, a high-tech company will simply terminate an existing American worker—typically, a more senior worker whose longtime service at the company has resulted in higher wages. Then, the company will use an H-1B visa to import a foreign replacement for that worker—one who accepts far lower wages and benefits, both because the wages in their home country are lower than what they are being offered on the H-1B temporary visa, and because their H-1B visa status is wholly controlled by the employer. That means that most foreign H-1B workers wouldn't dare ask for the same wages as their American counterparts because it would mean asking for equality from an employer who has the unilateral power to deport them.

The effects of this particular use of the H-1B visa are not surprising. As the Government Accountability Office noted, many high-tech "employers said that they hired H-1B workers in part because these workers would often accept lower salaries than similarly qualified U.S. workers." That is borne out by wage statistics from the U.S. Citizenship and Immigration Services agency, which the *New York Times* reports found that "the median salary for new H-1B holders in the information technology industry is actually about $50,000" as compared to much higher wages for similarly skilled domestic workers. And in case you believe President Obama's mind-boggling assertion that H-1B visas are "reserved only for those companies who say they cannot find somebody in (a) particular field," remember that his own Department of Labor admits the opposite is true: The visa may be used and "H-1B workers may be hired even when a qualified U.S. worker wants the job, and a U.S. worker can be displaced from the job in favor of the foreign worker."

As Hira reported in a study for the Economic Policy Institute, this straightforward use of the H-1B visa has easy to understand effects at some of America's biggest tech firms:

> In early 2009, Microsoft announced it would lay off 5,000 workers. After meeting that target by late 2009 it announced another round of 800 layoffs. Yet it continued to import H-1B workers, ranking fifth in FY08 [fiscal year 2008] and moving

up to second in FY09 on the top H-1B employers list. It received 2,355 H-1Bs in those two years alone. Microsoft also extensively contracts with leading offshore outsourcing firms like *Infosys and Satyam, which provide on-site personnel on guest worker visas.* In addition, it recently signed a major three-year contract with Infosys to "handle all the technology services and support for Microsoft itself." Given Infosys' statements in its SEC [Securities and Exchange Commission] filings, the vast majority of the workers servicing the Microsoft contract will almost surely be guest workers on H-1B and L-1 visas . . . Hewlett-Packard [HP] announced layoffs of nearly 25,000 employees after its acquisition of EDS in 2008, yet HP and EDS, and its offshore outsourcing subsidiary MPhasis, received 1,047 H-1Bs and L-1s in 2008 and 2009. Not all of those 25,000 jobs would be lost—approximately half of them were going to be offshored to workers in low-cost countries.

Of course, one of the most compelling arguments forwarded by proponents of the current H-1B program is that even though existing American employees are being put out of work by H-1B visa holders, at least these new arrivals to the United States might stay here, thus permanently adding their valuable high-tech skills to the overall American workforce. While that may be true for some of the H-1Bs who work directly for American firms, note the section in the above passage about foreign companies such as Infosys and Satyam, because it highlights that second, even more insidious way the H-1B program today operates—specifically, the way it works with non-American "consulting" firms.

Recall that such consulting firms' whole business is helping American high-tech firms *permanently* move various IT [information technology] services and operations overseas—not because workers in those countries are better skilled or educated, but because they will accept far lower wages and workplace standards. In this, we're not talking about Microsoft or HP hiring a few lower-wage fill-ins—we're talking about Microsoft or HP hiring an entire foreign firm like Infosys or Satyam to help them subcontract huge parts of their existing American business to foreign locales where wages are way lower, workplace regulations are lax, and unions do not exist. Once such contracts are in hand, these foreign subcontractors acquire thousands of H-1B visas from the U.S. government and dole them out to their own employees working on a contract basis inside major American high-tech firms inside the United States. Those employees are charged with helping those American firms permanently shift so-called "back office" services to low-wage locales like India. As the *New York Times* explained:

> (Indian outsourcing consultancy firms) have used (the H-1B visa) to further their primary mission, which is to gain the expertise necessary to take on critical tasks performed by Western companies, and perform them in India at a fraction of the cost. Thousands of H-1B visas every year are being won by individuals acting as outsourcing ambassadors. Highly skilled and easily meeting the objective standards for excellence that the law requires, the employees interact with U.S. companies like Morgan Stanley and Boeing, gathering an outsourcing mandate and lubricating the flow of tasks to an Indian back office. . . .

Offshoring US High-Tech

According to data compiled by *ComputerWorld*, this manipulation of the H-1B program is now one of the biggest ways the visa is used. As the trade magazine reported just three days before President Obama's public defense of the H-1B program, foreign "offshore outsourcing companies"—read: companies that subcontract huge swaths of domestic work to low-wage locales offshore—now "make up the majority of the top 10 H-1B visa users in 2011." This is why in a separate story, the *Times* went on to report that relatively few H-1B employees from offshore outsourcing firms seek permanent green cards. Far from the

H-1B being used in the way its proponents assert—as a method of attracting new, high-skilled workers to become permanent residents and thus improving America's overall high-tech workforce—the H-1B is now being used as a means of shipping America's entire high-tech industry offshore.

To be sure, it's impossible to know if President Obama is simply ignorant of these facts, or merely doesn't want to acknowledge them, for fear of alienating his campaign donors in the high-tech industry. But don't discount the power of those donors to turn an incumbent president into their own public advocate—especially during an election season when that incumbent president has a well-known history of relying on high-tech donors to underwrite his election campaigns. Obviously, those donors have a vested financial interest in answering Obama's fundraising call if—and when—that president seems determined to preserve the status quo and oppose any proposed pro-worker reforms of a program like the H-1B visa. After all, no matter if they are replacing domestic American workers with imported H-1B workers, or using the H-1B program to shift huge parts of their businesses offshore, those high-tech executives have a very lucrative scam going, and clearly, they don't care if American workers are the ultimate victims.

Whether the president cares remains an open question—but based on his comments about the H-1B program last week, his ultimate answer doesn't look promising.

Periodical and Internet Sources Bibliography

The following articles have been chosen to supplement the diverse views presented in this chapter.

Jagdish N. Bhagwati	"The Outsourcing Bogeyman," Council on Foreign Relations, August 23, 2011. www.cfr.org.
Boston Consulting Group	"Made in America, Again: Why Manufacturing Will Return to the U.S.," August 2011. www.bcg.com.
Adam Davidson	"Making It in America," *Atlantic*, January–February 2012.
Steve Denning	"Why Amazon Can't Make a Kindle in the USA," *Forbes*, August 17, 2011.
Charles Duhigg and Keith Bradsher	"How the U.S. Lost Out on iPhone Work," *New York Times*, January 21, 2012.
Thomas Heffner	"Outsourcing Our Future Wealth," *Economy in Crisis*, June 2, 2012. http://economyincrisis.org.
Paul McDougall	"Outsourcing or Automation: No Difference to Unemployed Workers," *Information Week*, March 28, 2012.
Michael Moran	"Analysis: After Decades of Outsourcing, Manufacturing Jobs Coming Home to US," *Global Post*, May 6, 2012. www.globalpost.com.
Ina Damm Muri	"Big Manufacturers More Likely to Support 'Made in USA,'" SmartPlanet, April 22, 2012. www.smartplanet.com.
David Sirota	"The 'Education Crisis' Myth," *Salon*, January 30, 2012. www.salon.com.
Jessica E. Vascellaro	"Tech Industry Rebuts Critics on Outsourcing," *Wall Street Journal*, June 6, 2012.

CHAPTER 4

How Should the US
Government Regulate
Outsourcing?

Chapter Preface

Nearly 20 percent of the Fortune 500 companies established in the United States between 1985 and 2010—including Google, Intel, eBay, and Yahoo!—were founded by immigrants. That number climbs to more than 40 percent if Fortune 500 companies founded by children of immigrants are included in the list.

These findings were included in a report called "The 'New American' Fortune 500," which was released by the Partnership for a New American Economy in June 2011. The report also reveals that these companies generate more than $4.2 trillion in annual revenue and employ more than 10 million people—an economic impact that "rivals the entire GDP [gross domestic product] of all but three nations."

The Partnership for a New American Economy is a bipartisan group of mayors and business leaders from all over the country who are working to raise awareness about the economic benefits of immigration reform. The group maintains that the economic prosperity that immigrants have brought to the United States is in jeopardy, primarily due to a "broken immigration system" that is "creating obstacles for existing businesses and driving new ones overseas."

To fix the system, members of the Partnership for a New American Economy advocate measures like granting permanent residency to foreign students who earn graduate degrees in STEM (science, technology, engineering, and math) fields, establishing a visa for foreign-born entrepreneurs who are interested in launching companies that would employ American workers, and raising or removing the limits on the number of H-1B temporary visas or guest worker permits for high-skilled foreign workers.

Others, however, are strongly opposed to the idea of expanding the H-1B visa program. In fact, a number of critics have charged that US corporations abuse the H-1B visa program and are not using it as it was originally intended. Corporations often maintain that hiring guest workers is necessary to combat a shortage of workers in certain occupations. But many critics say that such claims are bogus—that there are plenty of highly skilled workers in STEM fields on American soil. The problem, some say, is that corporations often merely claim they are unable to find enough skilled workers as justification for hiring foreign workers who will accept a lower wage than their American counterparts. Ron Hira, associate professor of public policy at the Rochester Institute of Technology and coauthor of *Outsourcing America: What's Behind Our National Crisis and How We Can Reclaim American Jobs* (2005), told the *Fort Worth Star-Telegram* in an April 2012 interview that he suspects that "about a third of H-1B use is probably on the up and up, about a third is now being used for offshore outsourcing, about a third is being used for low-cost workers." Hira—who has argued for reform of the H-1B visa program—has said that the current system has loopholes that allow employers to hire low-wage H-1B workers instead of American workers, who often are bypassed for open positions. Hira and other critics also have pointed out that corporations have used H-1B visas to replace existing American workers, who in some instances have had to train their foreign replacements. Some also have alleged that the current system has allowed corporations and offshore outsourcing firms to accelerate the offshoring of American jobs to lower-wage countries like India.

There are others who view the offshore outsourcing issue and the need for reform from an entirely different perspective. Some point to a flawed corporate tax structure, arguing that the US government needs to remove tax deductions for corporations that send jobs overseas and create new incentives for those that bring jobs back to American soil. Another group maintains that US policy makers need to encourage more exports and open up more overseas markets through trade agreements and other measures.

These ideas and others are highlighted in the viewpoints that follow. And while opinions and proposals vary widely, the issues and remedies outlined by these writers all appear to be aimed toward achieving the same goal: improving the health and long-term viability of the US economy.

> "To meet the needs of the U.S.
> economy and U.S. workers, the H-1B
> visa program needs immediate and
> substantial overhaul."

The US Guest Worker Visa Program Should Be Overhauled

Ronil Hira

Ronil Hira is an associate professor of public policy at the Rochester Institute of Technology in New York and coauthor of the 2005 book Outsourcing America: What's Behind Our National Crisis and How We Can Reclaim American Jobs. *In the following viewpoint, Hira argues that the H-1B visa program needs to be overhauled. As he points out, the H-1B visa program originally was intended to bring in foreign workers to complement the US workforce, not replace it. But according to Hira, program loopholes are allowing corporations to replace US workers with cheaper foreign ones. The United States benefits from the permanent immigration of high-skilled workers, Hira says, but extending the welcome to foreign workers should not happen at the expense of US workers.*

Ronil Hira, "H-1B Visas: Designing a Program to Meet the Needs of the US Economy and US Workers," Testimony Before the Subcommittee on Immigration Policy and Enforcement, Committee on the Judiciary, US House of Representatives, March 31, 2011.

As you read, consider the following questions:

1. According to Hira, what impact has the H-1B visa program had on companies that hire mostly American workers?
2. What are the four primary design flaws in the H-1B program, according to the author?
3. What are the ways that Hira suggests to resolve problems with the H-1B visa program?

I have concluded that the H-1B program, as currently designed and administered, does more harm than good. To meet the needs of the U.S. economy and U.S. workers, the H-1B visa program needs immediate and substantial overhaul.

The principal goal of the H-1B visa program is to bring in foreign workers who complement the U.S. workforce. Instead, loopholes in the program have made it too easy to bring in cheaper foreign workers, with ordinary skills, who directly substitute for, rather than complement, workers already in America. They are clearly displacing and denying opportunities to U.S. workers. A sizable share of highly skilled American workers and students—engineers, information technologists, and scientists—have concluded the H-1B program undercuts their wages and job opportunities. Those conclusions are largely correct and the program has lost legitimacy amongst much of America's high-tech workforce.

Furthermore, program loopholes provide an unfair competitive advantage to companies specializing in offshore outsourcing, speeding up the process of shipping high-wage, high-tech jobs overseas. It has disadvantaged companies that primarily hire American workers and forced those firms to accelerate their own offshoring, threatening America's future capacity to innovate and ability to create sufficient high-wage, high-technology jobs.

The "Outsourcing Visa"

For at least the past five years nearly all of the employers receiving the most H-1B are using them to offshore tens of thousands of high-wage, high-skilled American jobs. . . . Offshoring through the H-1B program is so common that it has been dubbed the "outsourcing visa" by India's former commerce minister.

The offshore outsourcing industry is adding hundreds of thousands of jobs every year. The top three India-based off-shore outsourcing firms, Tata Consultancy Services, Infosys, and Wipro, added a stunning 57,000 net new employees last year [2010] alone. If the H-1B program loopholes were closed, many of those jobs would have gone to Americans.

In a recent interview with *ComputerWorld* magazine, former Representative Bruce Morrison, a past chairman of this subcommittee and co-author of the Immigration Act of 1990 that created the H-1B program, summed up his view about how the H-1B program has been distorted by outsourcing:

> "If I knew in 1990 what I know today about the use of it [H-1Bs] for outsourcing, I wouldn't have drafted it so that staffing companies of that sort could have used it," Morrison said. Jobs are going abroad because of globalization, he said, "but the government shouldn't have its thumb on the scale, making it easier."

Below I summarize the problems with the H-1B program and how we can solve them.

Flaws Plague the H-1B Program

H-1B visa use has become antithetical to policy makers' goals due to four fundamental flaws:

Flaw 1—No labor market test. Contrary to popular perception in the media, and even amongst some policy makers, the H-1B visa program does not require any labor market test. In other words, employers are not required to show that qualified American workers are unavailable before hiring foreign workers through the H-1B visa program. Employers can and do bypass American workers when recruiting for open positions and even replace outright existing American workers with H-1B guest workers.

H-1B Employers Had Significant Offshoring Activity in 2007–2009

H-1B Use Rank	Company	H-1Bs Obtained FY 2007–2009	Significant Offshoring
1	Infosys	9,625	X
2	Wipro	7,216	X
3	Satyam	3,557	X
4	Microsoft	3,318	
5	Tata	2,368	X
6	Deloitte	1,896	
7	Cognizant	1,669	X
8	IBM	1,550	X
9	Intel	1,454	
10	Accenture	1,396	X

TAKEN FROM: Ronil Hira, "H-1B Visas: Designing a Program to Meet the Needs of the US Economy and US Workers," Testimony Before the Subcommittee on Immigration Policy and Enforcement, Committee of the Judiciary, US House of Representatives, March 31, 2011.

Flaw 2—Wage requirements are too low. Wage requirements are too low for H-1B visas and as a result the program is extensively used for wage arbitrage. Employers have told the Government Accountability Office (GAO) that they hire H-1Bs because they can legally pay below-market wages. The primary wage requirement is the setting of a wage floor, the lowest level an employer can pay an H-1B. The current wage floor is approximately the 17th percentile. A recent GAO study found that the majority (54%) of H-1B labor condition applications were for that lowest level, a level reserved for "entry level" positions, hardly a wage level that the "best and brightest" would earn. Just to provide one example of how low that wage can be, the Department of Labor has certified wages as low as $12.25 per hour for H-1B computer professionals, an occupation where the typical median wage is more than $70,000.

Flaw 3—Work permits are held by the employer. Visas are held by the employer rather than the worker. An H-1B worker's legal status in the country is thus dependent on the employer, giving inordinate power to the employer over the worker. As a result, H-1B workers can be easily exploited and put into poor working conditions, but they have little recourse because the working relationship is akin to indentured servitude. A number of cases have been highlighted in the press recently.

Flaw 4—The visa period is far too long. H-1B visas are issued for three years and are renewable for another three years, which magnifies the damage done by low wages and the inability of workers to change jobs freely. The visas can be extended indefinitely beyond six years when employers apply for permanent residence for their H-1B workers, keeping the visa valid beyond a decade in some cases. Extending the H-1B visa length in lieu of fixing the underlying problems associated with permanent residence creates more problems than it solves.

Flawed administration. In addition to the inherent flaws in the design of the program, there is little oversight or enforcement of the program.

H-1B program oversight and enforcement is deficient. The Department of Labor review of H-1B applications has been called a "rubber stamp" by its own Inspector General. And a 2008 DHS IG [Department of Homeland Security inspector general] report found that one-in-five H-1Bs were granted under false pretenses—either through outright fraud or serious technical violations. Critical data on actual program use is either not released or in some cases even collected. And program integrity largely relies on hope that H-1Bs would blow the whistle if they were being exploited. Whistle-blowing is highly unlikely given that H-1Bs' legal status depends on their continued employment.

Closing H-1B Visa Loopholes

By closing the H-1B visa loopholes described above, Congress would create and retain tens of thousands of high-wage American jobs and ensure that our labor market works fairly for American and foreign workers alike.

Institute an effective labor market test. An effective labor market test, such as labor certification for each application, needs to be created. U.S. workers should not be displaced by guest workers, and employers should demonstrate they have looked for and could not find qualified U.S. workers.

As a fix, some have proposed extending H-1B Dependent firm rules to all firms. But these rules are clearly not effective since H-1B Dependent firms are able to avoid hiring Americans while garnering thousands of H-1Bs annually.

Pay guest workers true market wages. Guest workers should be paid true *market* wages. The Congressionally imposed four-level wage structure should be abandoned. No guest worker should be paid less than the median wage in the occupation for all skill levels. Ensuring that employers pay market wages will remove the temptation of wage arbitrage. Further, employers should pay an annual fee equal to 10% of the average annual wage in the occupation. Those fees could be used to increase the skills of the American workforce and will ensure that employers are hiring guest workers who are filling real gaps in the labor market.

Limit the visa to a maximum of three years, with no renewal. This will ensure that employers either sponsor their H-1B workers for permanent residence or find a suitable American worker to fill the position.

Eliminate access to additional H-1B visas for any H-1B Dependent firms. The program is intended to help employers in the United States operate more effectively, providing them skilled workers they cannot find in the U.S. It should not be a way for businesses to compete here in the U.S. with an imported workforce. With the exception of very small businesses, no employer should be permitted to employ a workforce consisting of more than 15% H-1Bs. There is no reason, other than wage arbitrage, for any firm to have more than 15% of its workforce on guest worker visas.

Improved Transparency and Oversight

Shine light on H-1B program practice. There is widespread and substantial misunderstanding, in the media and even amongst some policy makers, about how the program works in practice. Many of these misunderstandings could be cleared up through greater transparency. Congress and USCIS [US Citizenship and Immigration Services] should publish data on program use by employer, including job title, job location, actual wages paid, and whether the worker is being sponsored for permanent residence. The data should include all H-1B workers, not just newly issued and renewed petitions.

Further, H-1B use by *H-1B Dependent* firms should be investigated and the findings publicly released. So called H-1B Dependent firms must meet additional requirements prior to hiring an H-1B worker, yet it is clear that these firms are able to circumvent Congress' intent regarding those additional requirements. As noted above these firms are able to hire literally thousands of H-1Bs annually without hiring any Americans for those positions.

Institute sensible oversight. Through their use of guest worker visas employers are asking government to intervene in the normal functioning of the American labor market. With this privilege should come accountability. Employers using guest workers should be subject to random audits to ensure they are fulfilling the obligations contained in their attestations. And Government agencies in charge of these programs—the Departments of Homeland Security, Labor, and State—should be granted the authority, and allocated resources, to ensure the programs are operating properly. Given the efforts in Congress to cut deeply into discretionary spending, some mechanism to fund these audits should be created. At a minimum, one in ten H-1B employers should be audited and, if they are not eliminated, every H-1B Dependent firm should be audited every year.

Establish a clear single objective for the H-1B program. The H-1B program is a so-called "dual-intent" visa; i.e., though the visas are temporary, employers can choose to sponsor these workers for permanent residence. While this design feature appears to provide flexibility, it comes at substantial cost. Is the H-1B program supposed to be truly temporary, be used sparingly, and only for short periods of time? Or is it the way to entice very recent foreign graduates of American universities to stay permanently? Or is it the primary bridge to immigration for high-skilled workers who are trained abroad? Each of these objectives creates inherent conflicts in program design; e.g., in setting wage floors. Congress should consider how to limit the scope of the H-1B program to improve its performance.

The H-1B is often equated with permanent residence in the media's discussion of high-skill immigration policy. As I have shown, with an analysis of the PERM [Program Electronic Review Management] database, many of the largest users of the H-1B program sponsor few, if any, of their H-1Bs for permanent residency. In the case of offshore outsourcing firm Tata Consultancy Services, it received 2,368 H-1Bs between 2007 and 2009, yet didn't sponsor a single H-1B for permanent residence. This example illustrates how the program's reality doesn't match the claims made by employer coalitions such as Compete America.

Problems with Other Programs

I understand that this hearing is specifically about the H-1B program but I would like to briefly highlight some other critical issues for high skill immigration policy that are directly related to the H-1B. Other temporary visa programs, such as the L-1 and B-1 and OPT [optional practical training], are also badly in need of an overhaul, and are being used to circumvent the annual numerical limit on H-1Bs. The L-1 visa program has even less control and oversight than the H-1B, has no annual "cap" and is very vulnerable to abuse. For example, the opportunities to exploit wage arbitrage using the L-1 is even greater than for the H-1B since the L-1 workers can be paid home country wages. The wage differentials between America and India, the source country for the largest share of L-1s, are staggering. With respect to the B-1 "business visitor" visa we have even less information about how it might be being exploited, but recent news reports and an ongoing lawsuit reveal that it is likely also being used to get around the H-1B rules and cap.

In 2008, the duration of the OPT work visa was extended for STEM [science, technology, engineering, and math] to 29 months without oversight or any approval from Congress. It appears that the largest beneficiaries of this extension are obscure colleges that are providing workers to the offshore outsourcing industry. There is no wage floor for OPT and one analyst estimate they are paid a mere 40% of what Americans earn. The rationale for the OPT extension has disappeared so it should be rolled back to its original duration.

And certain categories of high skill employment based permanent resident visa programs with very long backlogs should be cleared. A clear pathway to permanent residence, which can be completed in a reasonable amount of time, should be created.

Immigration, Not Trade Issues

Given the widespread use of both H-1B and L-1 visas by offshore outsourcing firms, Congress should take affirmative steps to make it clear that both guest worker programs and permanent residence are immigration, and not trade, policy issues. In 2003, the U.S. Trade Representative (USTR) negotiated free trade agreements (FTAs) with Chile and Singapore, which included additional H-1B visas for those two countries, and constrained Congress from changing laws that govern the L-1 visa program. In response, many members of Congress felt it was important to re-assert that Congress, not the USTR, has jurisdiction over immigration laws. But no law was ever passed. Without legislation, the muddying of trade and immigration policy will keep recurring. Most recently, it appears that some L-1 visa provisions were included as a side agreement in the Korea-U.S. Free Trade Agreement. Many countries, including India, have pressed for more liberalized visa regimes through trade agreements including proposing a new GATS [General Agreement on Trade in Services] work visa. Congress, not the U.S. Trade Representative, should have the authority to change these laws, and Congress should pass a law reaffirming jurisdiction.

A Standing Immigration Commission

A number of think tanks and academics, including the Migration Policy Institute and the Economic Policy Institute, have recommended that Congress create a standing commission on immigration. This commission would track the implementation of policy, the changing needs of the U.S. economy and labor market, and make recommendations to Congress on legislative changes. Given the nature of immigration policymaking Congress should seriously consider creating such a commission.

In conclusion, let me say that I believe the United States benefits enormously from high skilled permanent immigration, especially in the technology sectors. We can and should encourage the best and brightest to come to the United States and settle here permanently. But our future critically depends on our homegrown talent, and while we should welcome foreign workers, we must do it without undermining American workers and students. By closing the H-1B visa loopholes we would ensure that the technology sector remains an attractive labor market for Americans and continues to act as a magnet for the world's best and brightest.

The lobbyists supporting the H-1B program have repeatedly made claims that the program is needed because there is a shortage of American workers with the requisite skills, and the foreign workers being imported are the best and brightest. If that is indeed the case, then those employers should not object to these sensible reforms. The policies I have proposed pose no limitations on employers' ability to hire foreign workers who truly complement America's talent pool.

| *"High-skilled immigration reform legislation needs to promote . . . policies that enable access to the best and brightest talent from around the world."* |

The US Guest Worker Visa Program Needs to Be Expanded

TechAmerica Foundation

TechAmerica Foundation is a nonprofit organization that educates policy makers, opinion leaders, executives, and others about technology's impact on US competitiveness and economic growth. In the following viewpoint, the TechAmerica Foundation states that high-skilled foreign immigrants have given the United States a technological edge for decades, adding that temporary visa programs like H-1B help attract the best high-skilled foreign workers to this country. But according to the foundation, guest worker visa programs need to be reformed and expanded so that the United States can continue to attract high-skilled foreign nationals. US public policy, the TechAmerica Foundation asserts, also needs to support efforts to train more American workers for high-skill careers.

As you read, consider the following questions:
1. According to the author, why must foreign graduates of American universities often leave the country even though they have multiple job offers from US companies?
2. Of all the scientists and engineers in the United States, how many are foreign born, according to TechAmerica Foundation?
3. What are four myths about high-skilled immigrants and foreign nationals, according to the author?

Throughout our history, the United States has benefited from attracting many of the most talented minds on the planet. As a nation of immigrants, the United States found a winning formula; these emigrés pursued opportunities they could not find elsewhere and we as a country gained their entrepreneurship, intellect, hard work and skills, and the thousands of jobs they created in the United States.

Though much recent public debate has focused on unskilled, illegal immigration, an entirely different but essential category is often neglected: high-skilled, legal immigration.

Specific visa classifications have been created to attract the world's best and brightest to the United States. The most common are the H-1B and L-1, temporary visas that allow highly skilled foreign nationals to work in the United States for up to seven years. Employers who apply for an H-1B visa must not harm the working conditions of the current workforce, and they must pay the visa holder the prevailing or actual wage for that position (whichever is higher).

But is the system meeting the needs of an economy that is fueled by skills and innovation at a time when other countries are aggressively competing for the same talent?

Holders of H-1B and L-1 visas are often forced to leave the country because their green card[1] applications are not approved by the time their visas expire. Foreign graduates of American universities often cannot obtain visas or green cards to stay in the country, despite having multiple employment offers. And many in the pipeline to come to the United States simply choose to seek opportunities in countries where they feel more wanted.

They are confounded by the bureaucracy. The waits are too long and the regulations too inflexible. Foreign nationals of any single country can receive no more than seven percent of available green cards in a specific year. In effect this discriminates against individuals from populous nations that possess huge talent pools, like China and India.

A Threat to Security

If the best talent in the world cannot get into the United States, we face a true threat to our economic and national security. America's dirty little secret is that for decades high-skilled immigrants have been a critical safety valve for maintaining our technological preeminence. It is in our national self-interest to recognize their enormous contributions.

One of every four scientists and engineers in the United States is foreign-born. They fill our graduate schools and research labs. In terms of doctoral degrees, 54 percent of math degrees, 60 percent of computer science degrees, and 65 percent of engineering degrees awarded in the United States go to foreign nationals. Because they often pay full tuition, their financial support makes many graduate programs economically viable.

Many foreign graduates choose to stay—if they are allowed. They conduct the basic and applied scientific research that has so often formed the knowledge base for spinning off innovative products, companies, and industries.

The United States even benefits from those foreign nationals who do return home after graduation. These individuals become the political and business elites in their countries. Returning home with an American education, they retain positive impressions of the United States that foster strong friendships and linkages for a lifetime. In a tumultuous world, we cannot afford to lose these ties.

By deterring those who want to stay, we lose their intellectual abilities and innovations. We force our companies to follow them abroad. We lose the new companies, wealth, and thousands of high-paying jobs they would have created.

By kicking out tomorrow's Albert Einstein, Andy Grove [former CEO of Intel, born in Hungary], or Sergey Brin [cofounder of Google, born in Russia] , we help competing nations enhance their talented labor pools by chipping away at our own.

Myths About Foreign Nationals

Myth 1: Foreign nationals steal American jobs. In 2009, the private sector unemployment rate was 9.3 percent but the rate for computer and mathematical operations was just 5.4 percent and for electrical engineers 6.9 percent. High-tech companies are increasingly seeking skilled labor to feed a critical industry and cannot find it. Visit the website of many American technology companies and you will find thousands of unfilled, U.S.-based positions. Foreign nationals are critical for filling this void.

Not only do these individuals not take American jobs, they create them. Foreign-born immigrants are among this country's most prolific job creators. Co-founders from Google, eBay, Yahoo!, and hundreds of lesser known companies are foreign-born. Highly skilled, highly educated people create innovation. And innovation creates jobs.

Myth 2: Foreign nationals are paid less than American workers. Critics falsely contend that employers use the H-1B and L-1 programs to exploit cheap labor. They believe foreign nationals, desperate to remain in the United States, will accept lower than the market wage for their position. But the reality is that foreign visa holders are acutely aware of what they are worth and demand a competitive wage.

A report by the Center for Immigration Studies (CIS) concluded that H-1B computer programmers were paid less than their U.S. counterparts. The CIS researchers relied on what

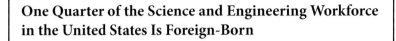

One Quarter of the Science and Engineering Workforce in the United States Is Foreign-Born

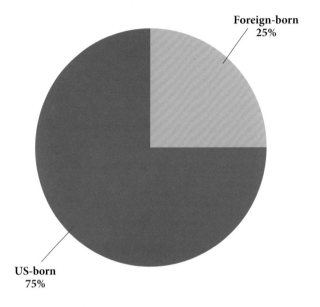

Foreign-born
25%

US-born
75%

TAKEN FROM: TechAmerica Foundation, "Attracting the Best and Brightest to the United States: Reforming High-Skilled Visa Policy," *Competitiveness Series*, vol. 36, March 2011, p. 3.

companies reported as the "prevailing wage" for those positions, instead of the actual wage paid. A 2006 report by the National Foundation for American Policy (NFAP) uncovered this methodological flaw and found that the actual wages paid to the programmers were 22 percent higher than the prevailing wage. NFAP also found that CIS vastly underestimated H-1B wages because it failed to control for age and work experience, as H-1B professionals tend to be younger than their American counterparts.

Further research conducted by the Center for Labor Market Studies at Northeastern University found that foreign-born and

American-born professionals earned virtually identical salaries in math and science fields.

The tech industry supports punitive measures against the small number of firms who have been found to exploit the system. The vast majority of companies play by the rules, pay market wages, and do not wish to see the integrity of the program called into question by a minority of infractors.

Myth 3: H-1Bs must stay with the employer who sponsored their visa and are therefore little more than indentured servants. Visa holders do not have to stay with the employer that sponsored them. They are free to seek employment elsewhere, provided their H-1B status has not expired.

As the NFAP study concluded, "Contrary to the myth that H-1B holders are 'indentured servants,' professionals on such visas understand their market value and show great mobility in the U.S. labor market." In surveying U.S. employers and immigration lawyers, NFAP found that H-1B workers change companies frequently, a conclusion supported by the Department of Homeland Security.

Myth 4: Visa holders do not pay income or Social security taxes. This myth is not raised as frequently as the others, but it exists. It is simply, and quite provably, false. Foreign visa holders are subject to the same taxes as U.S. citizens and permanent residents. Not only do they pay into the system, but because many are only here temporarily, they will never collect social security benefits. They are paying for benefits that they will not receive.

Support US and Foreign Workers

In the debate on competitiveness, many skeptics of high-skilled immigration argue that instead of encouraging more foreign nationals to come to the United States we should groom more Americans for these high-skilled careers.

The fact is that public policy should do both. These are not mutually exclusive paths to enhancing our competitiveness. They are complementary. The U.S. Bureau of Labor Statistics estimates the demand for technology jobs will grow 16 percent between 2008 and 2018.

Meanwhile, investment in educating the next generation of American-born science and technology workers is also lagging. Addressing it is a long-term project, one that is challenged by current budget crises at the state and local level. Skilled foreign nationals are needed now to fill a swelling number of highly technical and specialized positions.

Attracting this talent into the country facilitates companies' ability to maintain and expand operations in the United States. It brings the best and the brightest to us instead of forcing us to go to them. This is critical for ensuring a vibrant, competitive high-tech industry on our shores that will create high-paying jobs in the years to come.

Without the best and brightest international talent, the United States could never have developed the Manhattan Project [to develop nuclear weapons] or won the Space Race; we never could have created industry after innovative industry that is the source of so much of our wealth and prosperity.

The United States needs to compete aggressively for the world's best talent. America has been fortunate over the last sixty years; bright and innovative people had few alternative destinations for realizing their creativity. Now, countries around the world are cribbing from our playbook. They are investing in science and technology and attracting the talent that previously would have come to the United States.

Immigration Legislation

High-skilled immigration reform legislation needs to promote effective and transparent visa processing, adjudication, and reporting requirements. We believe the following principles should be considered to advance U.S. competitiveness:

- Promote policies that enable access to the best and brightest talent from around the world.

- Enable companies to continue investing in initiatives to develop the next generation of home grown workers, entrepreneurs, and high-tech developers essential for innovation and economic growth.

- Allow for Green Cards outside of the annual cap for foreign-born students who earn a graduate degree in STEM [science, technology, engineering, and math] fields from a U.S. college or university, so long as there is a job offer in the United States for the graduate in the field in which the degree was received.

- Repeal existing per-country limits on Green Cards.

- Reduce and prevent Green Card backlogs, including recapture of unused Green Cards, and exempting spouses and children from the annual Green Card caps.

- Enforce rules such as market-based wage and benefit requirements and displacement standards that protect American workers, promote U.S.-based investments, and facilitate global trade and U.S. exports.

- Grant exceptions to the H-1B cap to: shortage occupations; workers of extraordinary ability such as Nobel Prize winners; highly educated professionals who worked in the United States for three years prior to applying for an H-1B and have an advanced STEM degree; visa holders currently engaged in the Green Card process.

- Allow H-1B holders who have not violated their visa an automatic renewal that does not count against the cap.

- Allow L-1 professionals who have not violated their visa to have an automatic renewal.

- Establish sensible and transparent adjudication procedures and enforcement requirements that do not impose unreasonable costs on law-abiding companies, but that do punish companies that violate the system.

Note

1. A green card allows a foreign national to permanently live and work in the United States.

> "People have the right to know what
> companies are shipping jobs overseas,
> and what companies are committed
> to creating jobs for well-qualified
> Americans."

Legislation to Limit Outsourcing Is Essential and Effective

Jerry McNerney

Jerry McNerney, a Democrat, is the US representative from California's eleventh district. In the following viewpoint, a press release by McNerney's office outlines his efforts to bring more accountability to the outsourcing process through introduction of the Outsourcing Accountability Act of 2012. While the US House of Representatives voted the act down in March 2012, McNerney highlights some of the issues that he sees as flaws in the system. According to McNerney, it is difficult to tell whether corporations benefiting from tax incentives and other US policies are creating jobs on American soil or sending them overseas. In McNerney's view, corporations need to be held to a higher standard of accountability to the public and investors about their outsourcing activities.

Jerry McNerney, "McNerney Takes Lead on Outsourcing Bill," mcnerney.house.gov, January 31, 2012.

As you read, consider the following questions:

1. According to the author, what is the estimated number of jobs lost to offshoring every year?
2. Based on Bureau of Labor statistics cited in the viewpoint, how many occupations are susceptible to offshoring?
3. According to the author, what information must publicly traded companies disclose?

Today [January 31, 2012], Congressman Jerry McNerney (CA-11) joined Rep. Gary Peters (MI-09) and Rep. Tim Bishop (NY-01) in introducing the Outsourcing Accountability Act of 2012. The bill will require large corporations that have annual revenues of $1 billion or more to disclose how many of these employees are working domestically and how many are working abroad. This bill will bring transparency to corporate outsourcing practices and help close tax loopholes that send jobs overseas.

"Transparency is absolutely critical in making sure that we keep good jobs here in America. People have the right to know what companies are shipping jobs overseas, and what companies are committed to creating jobs for well-qualified Americans," said Rep. McNerney.

The Outsourcing Accountability Act will amend the Securities Exchange Act of 1934 so that any company required to file reports with the Securities and Exchange Commission must annually disclose both to the Commission and its shareholders the number of employees working domestically as compared to outside of the United States, as well as the percentage change from the previous year.

As the current law stands, it is difficult to gauge if corporations that benefit from tax incentives and other domestic policies are in fact generating jobs here at home, or sending them to other countries. The Outsourcing Accountability Act will hold them accountable for sending jobs overseas, and provide accurate information to people investing in the companies.

"In today's economy, we need to be focused on creating jobs and putting Americans to work. We must be committed to growing our economy to keep America competitive in the international market and ensuring that U.S. citizens have a path to finding good-paying jobs," said Rep. McNerney.

Outsourcing Has Taken a Toll

It is estimated that from 2000 to 2009, multinational corporations cut 2.9 million U.S. jobs while adding 2.4 million overseas. Annual job loss due to offshoring has been estimated to be around 300,000.

"When I go home every week, I hear stories from folks of how hard they are struggling in this economic climate. They tell me how difficult it is to find a good job that will allow them to support their families, and maybe set a little aside for their children's college education. We need to be focused on creating good, family wage jobs in America and stop sending jobs overseas," said Rep. McNerney.

- *Jobs Lost*: The *Washington Post* reports that between 2000 and 2009, multinational corporations cut 2.9 million U.S. jobs while adding 2.4 million overseas. In addition to job losses in the manufacturing sector, a study cited by the non-partisan Congressional Research Service estimates that as many as 3.4 million jobs in diverse sectors such as life sciences, architecture, and sales could have moved abroad by 2015. Annual job loss to offshoring has been estimated to be around 300,000, significantly slowing net job creation at a time when we need it most.

- *Jobs at Risk*: The Bureau of Labor Statistics estimates that of 515 distinct occupations, 160 may be susceptible to transfer offshore. In 2007, there were some 30 million jobs in these 160 offshorable service-providing occupations; they accounted for over one-fifth of total employment in that year.

More Transparency Is Needed

- *Current SEC [Securities and Exchange Commission] Reporting Requirements*: Publicly traded companies must disclose certain information in registration statements, prospectuses, and other periodic mandatory filings, including: a general description of the company's business, a description of the company's principal products and services, and a description of the company's subsidiaries. Companies must also disclose the total number of employees that they have and anticipated changes in the number of employees working in various corporate departments.

- *No Disclosure of Location of Employees*: Currently, corporations must disclose their total number of employees, but not where they are based. Elimination of 700 jobs in the U.S. and the creation of 1,000 jobs abroad would register only as a net gain of 300 jobs.

- *Policymakers*: With unemployment above 8% and persistently high unemployment rates predicted in the coming years, policymakers at every level of government must look at all credible options for creating jobs. Analyzing the effectiveness of past and future job creation policies is difficult without knowing whether corporations benefitting from tax incentives or other policies are creating jobs at home or abroad.

- *Investors*: Responsible investors have a right to know how publicly traded corporations are spending their money and whether they are hiring and investing in the U.S. or sending their earnings overseas. Where companies are hiring or laying off employees could be determinative, material information for potential investors.

- *Employees by Country and State*: The Outsourcing Accountability Act will add location of employees to annual SEC disclosure requirements. New reports must disclose the total number of employees in the U.S. broken out by State, as well as the total number of employees abroad broken out by country. The SEC is given the authority to issue regulations to implement this measure.

- *Change in Employees*: The Outsourcing Accountability Act will also require companies to report the percentage increase or decrease in employment numbers corresponding with each state and country.

- *Helping Consumers Buy American*: As we work to end the recession, consumers should have the right to know whether their hard earned dollars are supporting American jobs or not. Once this information becomes public, companies that employ more American workers than their competitors will have an economic incentive to advertise that they're supporting American jobs.

- *Common Sense Exemption for Recent Initial Public Offerings*: The legislation exempts companies for the first five years after their IPO [initial public offering] to avoid increasing compliance burdens on newly-public employers.

| *"Few bills that impact . . . offshoring are ever passed by Congress, and those few that are generally accomplish little."*

Limiting Outsourcing Through Legislation Does Not Work

Patrick Thibodeau

Patrick Thibodeau is a senior editor and writer who covers enterprise applications, outsourcing, government information technology (IT) policies, and IT workforce issues for Computerworld *and other publications. In the following viewpoint, Thibodeau argues that despite the public's increasing call for US policy makers to curb offshore outsourcing through legislation and increased regulation, such measures often are ineffective in changing the status quo. To bolster his argument, Thibodeau highlights several observations, including the fact that offshore outsourcing firms have historically adjusted to new regulations. Thibodeau also states that such legislation is not likely to change the overall trend toward increased outsourcing or federal officials' keen interest in exports, trade, and negotiating trade agreements with foreign countries.*

As you read, consider the following questions:

1. What piece of legislation does Thibodeau say offshore outsourcing firms fear the most?

2. What did former Ohio governor Ted Strickland do that generated bad press in India, according to the author?

3. As explained by Thibodeau, what are totalization agreements, and how do they apply to outsourcing?

Congress headed home this week to focus on midterm election campaigns, and offshore outsourcing is certain to be a topic of interest to many voters.

A just-released NBC News/*Wall Street Journal* poll of 1,000 people illustrates the strong interest in offshore outsourcing issues this year.

For instance, the poll asked whether respondents agreed with the statement, "U.S. companies are outsourcing much of their production and manufacturing work to foreign countries where wages are lower." The result: 68% strongly agreed, 18% somewhat agreed, 12% disagreed, and 2% were unsure.

But despite the growing public anger and calls for action in Washington, few bills that impact IT offshoring are ever passed by Congress, and those few that are generally accomplish little.

Here are five reasons why such proposals and legislation do little to change the status quo.

1. Offshore Firms Can Manage the Risk of New Laws

Congress recently approved a bill that raises H-1B application fees by $2,000 for companies where visa holders make up at least half of the total workforce.

U.S. Sen. Chuck Schumer (D-N.Y.) said the H-1B fee increase is aimed primarily at "a handful of foreign-controlled companies," including Wipro Technologies, Tata Consultancy Services and Infosys Technologies.

Indian officials denounced the bill and called it protectionist. But it isn't likely to change the H-1B strategies of the targeted Indian companies.

Infosys CFO V. Balakrishnan may have summed up the off-shore industry's view when he told investors that the visa fee increase, which could cost his company between $15 million and $20 million annually, "is manageable." Infosys is one of the largest users of H-1B visas: In 2008, it was approved for about 4,500 visas, up from 440 a year earlier.

2. Congress Hasn't Acted, and Isn't Expected to Act Soon, on the Bill Offshore Outsourcers Fear Most

The legislation most feared overseas is a bipartisan proposal from U.S. Sens. Chuck Grassley (R-Iowa) and Dick Durbin (D-Ill.) that includes a so-called 50-50 rule that would limit the number of workers on H-1B or L-1 visas to half of a firm's total U.S. head count.

Democratic leaders, so far, haven't pushed this bill, which remains in limbo.

Visa proponents in the U.S. and in India argue that the 50-50 restriction would prompt companies to send more work offshore, not less, though some offshore vendors are telling investors something different.

Wipro recently said that it plans to increase the percentage of locals in its U.S. workforce to 50% in the next two years. The company's Atlanta Development Center now has 500 employees. The new strategy would "reduce the overall dependence" on visas, Sabbudha Deb, Wirpo's chief global delivery officer, said in a recent conference call with investors.

Moreover, Wipro officials believe that hiring local workers could cut costs, because it eliminates the transportation, visa and other expenses associated with hiring Indian workers holding H-1B visas.

Infosys' Balakrishnan called the 50-50 rule a "worst-case option. If you don't have more than 50% locals, then you won't get any new visas," he told investors. Passage of the bill would probably lead the firm "to look at accelerating our local hiring," said Balakrishnan.

3. Exports and Trade Matter to State and Federal Government Officials

Ohio's Gov. Ted Strickland is a study in contrasts.

In July, the Ohio governor signed an agreement with Exhibitions India Group for up to $108,000 to promote the state "as a premier location" for direct investment and "an excellent place to do business," according to the contract provided to *Computerworld* by state development officials.

In August, Strickland banned offshore outsourcing by state agencies and received a mountain of bad press in India for his trouble.

It's worth pointing out that Strickland's hiring of an off-shore firm to promote Ohio was exempted from his executive order.

When asked by U.S. Trade Representative Ron Kirk to explain Ohio's position, Strickland said in a letter that "we are very well aware of the importance of trade and we highly value our trading partners. Ohio firms sold $381 million in goods, principally machinery, aircraft, and medical equipment, to Indian markets last year."

Nonetheless, Strickland is also taking on outsourcers during a difficult re-election campaign against Republican challenger John Kasich. Strickland has accused his opponent of being too close to Wall Street and a supporter of outsourcing.

4. No Legislation Is Likely to Change the Overall Trend Toward Outsourcing

The offshore industry generally adapts well to legislative changes that raise their costs. For example, some respond by increasing the hiring of workers in less costly countries, as well as in cities in India.

At the same time, the big offshore firms continue to grow at a phenomenal rate.

Tata Consultancy Services' latest plan calls for adding some 40,000 new employees during its current fiscal year—10,000 more than in its previous estimate. Tata, which now employs about 160,000 workers, said its revenues in the June 2010 quarter increased by 6.4% sequentially and 21.2% year-to-year. Rival Infosys reported that its revenues in the same period grew by 4.8% sequentially and 21% year-to-year.

Outsourcing firms in the U.S., such as Teaneck, N.J.–based Cognizant Technology Solutions, which uses offshore labor, are also doing well. In August, Cognizant reported second-quarter revenue that was up 15% sequentially and 42% from the year-ago quarter.

5. As Congress Debates Laws, Federal Government Officials Work on Trade Agreements

Indian and U.S. negotiators have been meeting in advance of President Obama's visit to India, which is scheduled for right after the November elections.

The negotiating teams are working toward a totalization agreement, which would exempt Indian firms from having to pay Social Security and Medicare taxes on temporary visa workers. H-1B visas workers who pay these taxes will never receive any benefit from them unless they become permanent residents. Such a law could cut the firms' H-1B labor costs by up to 14%.

The U.S. has similar totalization agreements with other countries, mostly in Europe. The Indian government has also reached agreements with European nations and expects to sign one soon with Canada. If a similar tax-break agreement is reached with the U.S., the overall benefit from this program may more than offset the cost of any increase in H-1B visas fees.

Periodical and Internet Sources Bibliography

The following articles have been chosen to supplement the diverse views presented in this chapter.

Patrick Brennan	"Playing Politics with Protectionism," *National Review*, May 16, 2012.
Jonette Christian	"Not Enough Smart Americans? Don't Buy It," *Bangor Daily News*, June 21, 2012.
Donna Conroy	"While Shaking Hands at Obama's 'Insourcing Jobs' Forum, GalaxE Outsourcing to India too," *Daily Kos*, January 19, 2012. www.daily kos.com.
David Dapice	"Tax Reform May Not Bring US Jobs Back," YaleGlobal Online, February 3, 2012. http://yaleglobal .yale.edu.
Matthew Dunn	"Drive Business Back to the U.S., Reform H-1B Visa Laws," *Forbes*, June 19, 2012.
Ron Hira	"H-1B Workers Are in a State of Indentured Servitude," *U.S. News & World Report*, December 28, 2011.
Stephanie Moore	"True Global Outsourcing Should End the Visa Debate," *Forbes*, April 10, 2012.
Scott Paul	"OUT: Outsourcing. IN: Insourcing," *Huffington Post*, January 12, 2012. www.huffingtonpost.com.
Eve Tahmincioglu	"Obama's Insourcing Jobs Plan Faces an Uphill Battle," MSNBC, January 25, 2012. www.msnbc.com.
Wall Street Journal	"Visa Protectionism," April 12, 2012.
White House	"President Obama's Blueprint to Support U.S. Manufacturing Jobs, Discourage Outsourcing, and Encourage Insourcing," January 25, 2012. www.whitehouse.gov.

For Further Discussion

Chapter One

1. Ed Frauenheim argues in his viewpoint that offshore outsourcing can lead to exploitation of workers. To back his argument, he cites reports of harsh, dangerous working conditions at Chinese factories where Apple products are manufactured. In his viewpoint, he also points out that American consumers seem to care more about buying a new iPhone than working conditions in China. And yet even as he makes these arguments, Frauenheim admits that he has owned a series of Mac laptops and that he is listening to an iPod while writing the actual viewpoint. Given this information, do you think Frauenheim's arguments about offshore outsourcing are less convincing or more convincing? Does the fact that he uses Apple products negate his argument that outsourcing can lead to the exploitation of workers? Explain your answer.

2. The Monitor Company Group and Leila Janah both highlight the benefits of offshore outsourcing and how it can help lift people in some of the most impoverished regions of the world out of poverty. Janah is the CEO of a nonprofit called Samasource, which hires people from impoverished regions of the world to perform micro-tasks via computer work for companies. The Monitor Company Group viewpoint, on the other hand, was compiled following 120 interviews with a wide range of people in thirteen countries as well as twenty-five industry experts. Which viewpoint makes a more convincing argument for the benefits of offshore outsourcing? Why?

Chapter Two

1. In this chapter, Sarah Murray argues that outsourcing can foster innovation. By contrast, Stephanie Overby of

CIO highlights the views of two Harvard Business School professors who point out that companies can irreversibly harm their competitiveness and ability to innovate by off-shoring work. Murray's viewpoint is sponsored by a company called Siemens PLM Software, whereas Overby's article appears in a trade magazine that is published for technology and business leaders. From an objectivity standpoint, does it matter that a software company sponsored Murray's report or that Overby's viewpoint appeared in a trade publication for technology and business leaders? Would you feel any different about the objectivity of the information presented if both viewpoints were published in a *New York Times* article or by another media outlet? Why or why not? How is it possible to tell whether information is biased or not, and is it always possible to tell?

2. In this chapter, a management consulting company and a reporter explore the potential results of outsourcing on corporate profits. The viewpoint by Capgemini Consulting is based on a survey of company executives. The viewpoint by Michael Hiltzik reports on the experience of particular company, Boeing, with a major project that relied on outsourcing. What motivation or agenda did the authors have to write their respective viewpoints? Which viewpoint presents a more convincing argument? Are either or both viewpoints objective in their analyses? Is objectivity needed to accurately examine corporate profitability? Why or why not?

Chapter Three

1. Paul Craig Roberts and Michael Newkirk explore the impact that outsourcing has had on the US economy. In your opinion, which viewpoint presents the most convincing and the least convincing arguments? What are the characteristics of a convincing report or article, in your opinion? Do you think it is possible to write about an issue while also remain-

ing completely unbiased? Which viewpoint seems most objective and which seems to be the most biased? Explain your answer with examples from each viewpoint.

2. Paul Craig Roberts claims that corporate outsourcers have published "misleading one-sided studies" to convince people of the benefits of outsourcing. Are there any studies cited or included in this chapter that seem to fit Roberts's description? What about in other chapters of this book? In his viewpoint, Roberts also states that very few have looked objectively at the issue of outsourcing. Do you think Roberts's viewpoint takes an objective, unbiased look at outsourcing? Why or why not?

Chapter Four

1. Ronil Hira and TechAmerica Foundation, in their respective viewpoints, make arguments for changes that should be made to the H-1B guest worker program. Do the authors of each viewpoint argue for more or for less governmental regulation? Which viewpoint makes the most convincing argument for how the H-1B program should be addressed? What methods does each viewpoint use to strengthen its position? Explain your answers with specific examples from each viewpoint.

2. What is the primary argument behind the outsourcing legislation that Jerry McNerney and a couple of other lawmakers proposed in the McNerney viewpoint? By contrast, what is the main argument behind Patrick Thibodeau's viewpoint? Which viewpoint presents a more convincing argument? Why? Do you think it is possible to make companies more transparent and accountable through legislation? Why or why not?

Organizations to Contact

The editors have compiled the following list of organizations concerned with the issues debated in this book. The descriptions are derived from materials provided by the organizations. All have publications or information available for interested readers. The list was compiled on the date of publication of the present volume; names, addresses, phone and fax numbers, and e-mail and Internet addresses may change. Be aware that many organizations take several weeks or longer to respond to inquiries, so allow as much time as possible.

American Federation of Labor and Congress of Industrial Organizations (AFL-CIO)
815 Sixteenth Street NW
Washington, DC 20006
(202) 637-5000
website: www.aflcio.org

The AFL-CIO is a voluntary membership organization of fifty-six national and international labor unions that represents 12.2 million working people from a wide range of professions. The organization seeks to protect workers in the global economy and works to keep jobs at home by supporting changes to trade and other policies that impact workers. The AFL-CIO offers a number of reports, fact sheets, and documents on its website about outsourcing and other issues.

Cato Institute
1000 Massachusetts Ave. NW
Washington, DC 20001
(202) 842-0200 • fax: (202) 842-3490
website: www.cato.org

The Cato Institute is a think tank and public policy research organization that focuses on issues involving individual liberty, limited government, and free markets. The organization has published a number of articles and papers supporting outsourcing as a means of strengthening the US economy and creating jobs. In addition to providing articles, op-ed pieces, blog posts, multimedia, and other resources on its website, the Cato Institute publishes several books every year, as well as publications such as the *Cato Journal, Cato's Letters*, the *Cato Policy Report*, white papers, policy analyses, and various bulletins.

Citizens for Tax Justice
1616 P Street NW, Suite 200
Washington, DC 20036
(202) 299-1066 • fax: (202) 299-1065
e-mail: ctj@ctj.org
website: www.ctj.org

The Citizens for Tax Justice is a public interest research and advocacy organization that works to give citizens a greater voice on issues related to local, state, and federal taxes. In recent years, the organization has spoken out about offshore tax abuses and other related offshoring issues. Through its website, Citizens for Tax Justice provides reports, fact sheets, updates on changes in state and federal tax laws and legislation, and regular commentary about various tax issues in the "Tax Justice Digest" page of the site.

Council on Foreign Relations (CFR)
58 E. Sixty-Eighth Street
New York, NY 10065
(212) 434-9400 • fax: (212) 434-9800
e-mail: communications@cfr.org
website: www.cfr.org

The Council on Foreign Relations is an independent, nonpartisan membership think tank and publisher that seeks to inform its members, government officials, members of the media, civic and religious leaders, and business executives about foreign policy issues facing the United States and other countries. While the organization does not take formal positions on policy matters, it does provide a forum for a diverse range of scholars and officials on various foreign policy issues. CFR has published a number of reports and articles about outsourcing—especially pertaining to US trade policy. The organization publishes a bimonthly magazine called *Foreign Affairs*, which has a related website that publishes daily features on a wide range of foreign policy issues. The CFR website also includes op-ed pieces, videos, podcasts, background documents, blogs, analysis pieces, and interviews.

Economic Policy Institute (EPI)
1333 H Street NW, Suite 300, East Tower
Washington, DC 20005-4707
(202) 775-8810 • fax: (202) 775-0819
e-mail: epi@epi.org
www.epi.org

The Economic Policy Institute is a nonpartisan think tank that works to broaden the public debate about strategies that can help create a fair, prosperous economy. It conducts research, analysis, and proposes policies to educate citizens, and protect and improve economic conditions for low- to middle-income US workers. Trade, globalization, and outsourcing are among the economic policy issues that EPI addresses in its research papers and policy analyses. In particular, EPI has underscored the effect of international trade agreements on workers and the importance of including enforceable labor standards in such agreements. Along with providing a wide range of articles and multimedia resources on its website, EPI also has published resources such as the *State of Working America*.

The Heritage Foundation
214 Massachusetts Ave. NE
Washington, DC 20002-4999
(202) 546-4400 • fax: (202) 546-8328

e-mail: info@heritage.org
website: www.heritage.org

The Heritage Foundation is a think tank that focuses on developing and promoting conservative public policies based on principles such as free enterprise, individual freedom, limited government, and traditional American values. The foundation publishes a great deal of commentary on its website in support of outsourcing and free trade agreements, arguing that offshoring benefits the US economy through job creation and investment. With published commentary, blog posts, fact sheets, and multimedia resources provided on its website, the foundation also works to dispel common perceptions that cast outsourcing in a negative light.

National Bureau of Economic Research (NBER)
1050 Massachusetts Ave.
Cambridge, MA 02138
(617) 868-3900
e-mail: info@nber.org
website: www.nber.org

The National Bureau of Economic Research is a private, nonprofit, nonpartisan research organization that disseminates unbiased economic research among policy makers, business professionals, and the academic community. The organization publishes reports, statistics, and working papers that cover a number of topics, including offshore outsourcing, the US labor market, globalization, trade agreements, and other outsourcing-related issues. The NBER also provides online content from various print publications, including the monthly *NBER Digest*, the quarterly *NBER Reporter*, and the quarterly *Bulletin on Aging and Health*.

Peterson Institute for International Economics
1750 Massachusetts Ave. NW
Washington, DC 20036

(202) 328-9000 • fax: (202) 659-3225
e-mail: comments@piie.com
website: www.piie.org

The Peterson Institute for International Economics is a private, nonprofit, nonpartisan research institution that focuses on international economic policy. The institute works to provide neutral analysis and solutions to a broad range of international economic problems. With regard to outsourcing, the institute publishes reports that explore both sides of the issue, as well as the impact that outsourcing has on individuals, corporations, and the US economy as a whole. These reports, along with a wide range of commentary, speeches, papers, congressional testimony, blogs, and policy briefs are accessible on the institute's website.

Progressive Policy Institute (PPI)
1101 Fourteenth Street NW, Suite 1250
Washington, DC 20005
(202) 525-3926 • fax: (202) 525-3941
website: www.progressivepolicy.org

The Progressive Policy Institute is an organization that promotes a progressive perspective on a broad range of public policy issues that support international and political freedom. The institute has launched an online think tank and web-based research center called ProgressiveFix.com that solicits and coordinates written work from a wide range of experts. PPI publications and content typically focus on the benefits of outsourcing and advocate policies that support trade expansion, fight protectionism, improve the United States' global competitiveness, and provide American families with the means to achieve economic success and security. In addition to published articles on the organization's website, PPI also offers e-newsletters, op-ed pieces, press releases, and other resources.

Reason Foundation

3415 S. Sepulveda Blvd., Suite 400
Los Angeles, CA 90034
(310) 391-2245 • fax: (310) 391-4395
website: http://reason.org

The Reason Foundation is a nonprofit libertarian research organization that conducts public policy research on a wide variety of issues and also advocates free markets, individual freedoms, and other libertarian-oriented policies and principles. On the subject of outsourcing, the foundation's published reports and other materials focus on the benefits—such as insourcing of jobs and increased productivity—that outsourcing provides to US companies and workers. The foundation publishes a print magazine called *Reason*, a bimonthly journal called *Privatization Watch*, along with a number of other publications. Through its website, the foundation also publishes policy research, commentary, op-eds, testimony, e-newsletters, news items, and other resources on outsourcing and a broad range of other issues.

The Rockefeller Foundation

420 Fifth Ave.
New York, NY 10018
(212) 869-8500 • fax: (212) 764-3468
website: www.rockefellerfoundation.org

The Rockefeller Foundation was established by John D. Rockefeller Sr. in 1913 to promote the well-being of people all over the globe. Today, the foundation funds initiatives that support "smart globalization" efforts that provide people with greater access to assistance with social, economic, health, and environmental challenges. Where outsourcing is concerned, the foundation has funded research, development, and testing of business models that help alleviate poverty by employing socioeconomically disadvantaged people worldwide. Through this practice—known as impact sourcing—companies benefit from high-quality services at competitive prices, while also providing help and support to individuals and communities most in need economically. The foundation also funds initiatives and research that help support and protect US workers. Through its website, the Rockefeller Foundation supplies a number of reports, speeches, presentations, news items, press releases, and videos on a wide range of issues, including outsourcing, globalization, and fair trade.

United Steelworkers (USW)
Five Gateway Center
Pittsburgh, PA 15222
(412) 562-2400
website: www.usw.org

The United Steelworkers is the largest industrial labor union in North America. With members in the United States, Canada, and the Caribbean, the USW represents workers in a wide range of industries, including primary and fabricated metals, chemicals, rubber, pharmaceuticals, health care, and several others. On the issue of outsourcing, the USW believes that US workers and their families are negatively impacted by what the union believes to be predatory and unfair trade practices of several countries, including China. The USW also is critical of corporations and policies that support offshoring jobs—a practice that the USW believes harms US workers by shipping jobs overseas. Through its website, the USW provides a wide variety of publications, including e-newsletters such as *USW@Work* and *FrontLines*, as well as numerous reports, white papers, blog posts, testimony, news advisories, and videos.

US Chamber of Commerce
1615 H Street NW
Washington, DC 20062-2000
(800) 638-6582
website: www.uschamber.com

The US Chamber of Commerce is a business advocacy organization that represents the interests of more than 3 million businesses and corporations throughout the United States. The US Chamber advocates policies that strengthen US competitiveness worldwide and is supportive of efforts to increase exports, expand trade, and encourage openness to foreign investment, immigrants, and international visitors. The organization also has argued that outsourcing has increased the efficiency of manufacturing processes, lowered costs to consumers, and has benefited US workers, the economy, and corporations. On its website, the US Chamber provides access to a wide range of reports, commentary, op-eds, news advisories, testimony, and other resources on a wide range of issues, including those related to outsourcing.

US Department of Commerce
1401 Constitution Ave. NW
Washington, DC 20230
(202) 482-4883 • fax: (202) 482-5168
website: www.commerce.gov

The US Department of Commerce works to promote job creation, economic growth, sustainable development, and an improved standard of living for US citizens by working with businesses, communities, the academic community, and workers. In support of this mission, the US Department of Commerce acts to strengthen US competitiveness in the global marketplace, advocating increased exports, a strong manufacturing sector, and global trade agreements that open up markets for US goods and services. Through its website, the US Department of Commerce provides a broad range of statistical data, fact sheets, reports, commentary and op-ed pieces, speeches, blog posts, and other resources about a wide variety of issues related to outsourcing.

Bibliography of Books

Jennifer Baum

Small Business Outsourcing: From Detroit to Delhi. Royal Oak, MI: Scribe, 2011.

Jagdish N. Bhagwati

In Defense of Globalization. New York: Oxford University Press, 2007.

Jagdish N. Bhagwati, Alan S. Blinder, and Benjamin M. Friedman

Offshoring of American Jobs: What Response from U.S. Economic Policy? Cambridge, MA: Massachusetts Institute of Technology Press, 2009.

Sara Bongiorni

A Year Without "Made in China": One Family's True Life Adventure in the Global Economy. Hoboken, NJ: John Wiley & Sons, 2008.

Jack Buffington

An Easy Out: Corporate America's Addiction to Outsourcing. Westport, CT: Praeger, 2007.

Farok J. Contractor, Vikas Kumar, Sumit K. Kundu, and Torben Pedersen

Global Outsourcing and Offshoring: An Integrated Approach to Theory and Corporate Strategy. Cambridge, UK: Cambridge University Press, 2012.

Joseph Dillon Davey

The Shrinking American Middle Class: The Social and Cultural Implications of Growing Inequality. New York: Palgrave Macmillan, 2012.

Lou Dobbs	*Exporting America: Why Corporate Greed Is Shipping American Jobs Overseas.* New York: Warner Business, 2006.
Byron L. Dorgan	*Take This Job and Ship It: How Corporate Greed and Brain-Dead Politics Are Selling Out America.* New York: St. Martin's, 2007.
Diana Farrell	*Offshoring: Understanding the Emerging Global Labor Market.* Boston: Harvard Business School, 2006.
Robert C. Feenstra	*Offshoring in the Global Economy: Microeconomic Structure and Macroeconomic Implications.* Cambridge, MA: Massachusetts Institute of Technology Press, 2010.
Ian Fletcher	*Free Trade Doesn't Work: What Should Replace It and Why.* Washington, DC: U.S. Business and Industry Council, 2010.
Jody Freeman and Martha Minow	*Government by Contract: Outsourcing and American Democracy.* Cambridge, MA: Harvard University Press, 2009.
Ron French	*Driven Abroad: The Outsourcing of America.* Muskegon, MI: RDR, 2006.
Steven Greenhouse	*The Big Squeeze: Tough Times for the American Worker.* New York: Knopf, 2008.

Daniel T. Griswold

Mad About Trade: Why Main Street America Should Embrace Globalization. Washington, DC: Cato Institute, 2009.

Ron Hira and Anil Hira

Outsourcing America: The True Cost of Shipping Jobs Overseas and What Can Be Done About It. New York: AMACOM, 2008.

Douglas A. Irwin

Free Trade Under Fire, third ed. Princeton, NJ: Princeton University Press, 2009.

J. Bradford Jensen

Global Trade in Services: Fear, Facts, and Offshoring. Washington, DC: Peterson Institute for International Economics, 2011.

Robert E. Kennedy and Ajay Sharm

The Services Shift: Seizing the Ultimate Offshore Opportunity. Upper Saddle River, NJ: Pearson Education, 2009.

Jacob Funk Kirkegaard

The Accelerating Decline in America's High-Skilled Workforce: Implications for Immigration Policy. Washington, DC: Peterson Institute for International Economics, 2007.

Thomas M. Koulopoulos and Tom Roloff

Smartsourcing: Driving Innovation and Growth Through Outsourcing. Avon, MA: Platinum Press, 2006.

Robert Z. Lawrence — *Blue-Collar Blues: Is Trade to Blame for Rising US Income Inequality?* Washington, DC: Peterson Institute for International Economics, 2008.

Todd Lipscomb — *Re-made in the USA: How We Can Restore Jobs, Retool Manufacturing, and Compete with the World.* Hoboken, NJ: John Wiley & Sons, 2011.

Andrew Liveris — *Make It in America: The Case for Re-inventing the Economy.* Hoboken, NJ: John Wiley & Sons, 2011.

Paul Midler — *Poorly Made in China: An Insider's Account of the China Production Game.* Hoboken, NJ: John Wiley & Sons, 2009.

Shezhad Nadeem — *Dead Ringers: How Outsourcing Is Changing the Way Indians Understand Themselves.* Princeton, NJ: Princeton University Press, 2011.

Peter W. Navarro and Greg Autry — *Death by China: Confronting the Dragon—a Global Call to Action.* Upper Saddle River, NJ: Pearson Education, 2011.

Eva Paus — *Global Capitalism Unbound: Winners and Losers from Offshore Outsourcing.* New York: Palgrave Macmillan, 2007.

Scott Phillips	*The Moral Case on Outsourcing: How Good, Bad, or Ugly Is It for America and the World?* Portland, OR: Alitum, 2012.
Clyde Prestowitz	*The Betrayal of American Prosperity: Free Market Delusions, America's Decline, and How We Must Compete in the Post-Dollar Era.* New York: Free Press, 2010.
Paul Craig Roberts	*How the Economy Was Lost: The War of the Worlds.* Oakland, CA: AK Press, 2010.
Andrew Ross	*Fast Boat to China: High-Tech Outsourcing and the Consequences of Free Trade; Lessons from Shanghai.* New York: Vintage Books, 2007.
Allison Stanger	*One Nation Under Contract: The Outsourcing of American Power and the Future of Foreign Policy.* New Haven, CT: Yale University Press, 2009.
Atul Vashistha and Avinash Vashistha	*The Offshore Nation: Strategies for Success in Global Outsourcing and Offshoring.* New York: McGraw-Hill, 2006.
Kate Vitasek, Mike Ledyard, and Karl B. Manrodt	*Vested Outsourcing: Five Rules That Will Transform Outsourcing.* New York: Palgrave MacMillan, 2010.

Index

employment gains, 77
foreign direct investment (FDI)
and, 89–90
India and, 87
negative effects of outsourcing,
83
tradable services, 95, 97
US and, 87
US citizen job losses, 82, 100,
136
US manufacturing statistics
2008, 90
See also Outsourcing; Taxes
Massachusetts General Hospital,
54
McCarty, Tom, 74
McDonnell-Douglas, 72, 73
McKinsey Global Institute, 84–
85
McNerney, Jerry, 134–138
Medical services, 82
Medicare taxes, 143
Metz, Bill, 51–52
Mexico, 78, 84
Michigan, 45
Micro-task outsourcing, 33, 36
Microsoft, 105–107
Migration Policy Institute, 123
MIT Sloan School of Management,
54
Mobile communications industry,
59–60
Monitor Company Group, 22–27
Morgan Stanley, 107
Morrison, Bruce, 116
MPhasis, 106
Mulally, Alan, 72
Multinational corporations
(MNCs), 89–90
Murray, Sarah, 47–63
Muthee, Steve, 34, 36–37

N
National Association of
Manufacturers (NAM), 87
National Foundation for American
Policy (NFAP), 129, 130
NBC News, 140
New York Times (newspaper), 20,
29–31, 105
Newkirk, Michael, 86–91
News reporting, 82
NGOs (nongovernmental organi-
zations), 26
Nike Inc., 30
Northeastern University, 129–130

O
Obama, Barack
economic policy failures, 18
India visit, 143
misuse of H-1B program and,
107–108
outsourcing and, 14–17
visa programs and, 103–105
oDesk, 39–42
Ohio, 17, 142
Open Business Models
(Chesbrough), 49
Open Innovation (Chesbrough), 49
OPT (optional practical training),
122
Outsourcing
attrition, 35
back office services, 107
benefits, 22–27
BPO (business process outsourcing), 23–27
cost reductions, 45–46, 50, 60,
64–68
downsizing and, 71
economic reform and, 18
efficiency and, 46, 50
exploitation and, 28–31